2020 VISI

Liberalism and Gl

John Alderdice
Lone Dybkjaer
Pere Esteve
Werner Hoyer
Anne Jensen
Lousewies van der Laan
Cecilia Malmström
Annemie Neyts-Uyttebroeck
Graham Watson
Jan-Kees Wiebenga

Compiled and Edited by
GRAHAM WATSON MEP
& Howard Mollett

CENTRE FOR REFORM

London

Published in September 2001 by:
Centre for Reform
Dean Bradley House, 52 Horseferry Road
London SW1P 2AF
United Kingdom

Tel: 020 7222 5121
Fax: 020 7222 5185
E-mail: info@cfr.org.uk
Website: www.cfr.org.uk

ISBN 1-902622-26-X
ISSN 1463-6751

Printed by
Contract Printing,
1 St. James Road,
St. James Industrial Estate,
Corby, Northants. NN18 8AL.
United Kingdom

Contents

Foreword

The idea of inviting fellow Liberals to contribute to a collection of essays such as this lodged itself in my mind in the early part of last year when I was thinking about the relevance of Liberalism to humankind in a new century. Towards the end of last year I approached a number of colleagues, soliciting contributions. The outcome, as with most human endeavour, is far from perfect. I would have liked and should have sought more vigorously contributions from some not represented here, particularly politicians from outside western Europe. I might usefully have been more precise at the outset in my guidance to contributors. Nonetheless, I am exceedingly grateful to the four men and five women who accepted my invitation to write. They have been gracious in the face of my exhortations and indulgent of my demands. Their chapters make good reading alone; in combination with others, they provide a cameo of Liberal ideas at the turn of the third Christian millennium and help to chart a course for those adhering to Liberal beliefs.

David Miliband, one of the architects of the UK Labour Party's 'Third Way', replied rather weakly to a garrulous question of mine at a prestigious London dinner circle a couple of years ago with the words 'politicians may no longer write books, but they still read them'. One of the joys of working with Liberal parliamentarians is their willingness, despite many other demands on their time and energies, to commit their ideas to paper and hence to detailed public scrutiny. It is perhaps a comment on the fate of the much-trumpeted Third Way that while most of this volume's authors mention it, few devote much consideration to it. What none omits, however, is a reflection on the significant and sometimes tragically violent public protests which increasingly accompany international meetings of national leaders who are predominantly social democrat adherents to the so-called Third Way.

I am indebted to my co-editor Howard Mollett, currently working with Friends of the Earth, for the work he has done on this collection of essays; and to my Brussels-based assistant Sarah Kent, for whom the demands of preparing a pamphlet for publication during the month of August have been little short of a baptism of fire. Both have been industrious and conscientious. The ELDR Group of the European Parliament has been generous in its assistance. Anthony Rowlands and his colleagues at the Centre for Reform have once again been indulgent of my idiosyncrasies and generous in their advice. Any profits from this work will go to assisting them in the publication of other Centre for Reform texts.

My wife Rita has again allowed our summer holiday to be disrupted by the work involved in the compilation of this second collection of essays in two years with the generosity of spirit which only a fellow Liberal could offer. Her dedication is beyond financial reward.

To all those who have helped, I am grateful. I hope those who buy this book find it interesting reading.

Graham Watson
September 2001

Notes on the Contributors

John, Lord Alderdice joined the Alliance Party of Northern Ireland in 1978, becoming Party Leader nine years later and led the Alliance Party through the Multi-Party Talks, which produced the Good Friday Agreement. Following his role in the Peace Process, he was a joint recipient of the Kennedy Profile in Courage Award in 1999. He is Vice President of the ELDR Party, and currently holds the position of Speaker in the Northern Ireland Assembly.

Lone Dybkjær MEP is the ELDR coordinator of the Committee on Women's Rights and Equal Opportunities, as well as being first Vice President of the Committee on Development and Cooperation ACP/EU. She is a member of the ELDR bureau. Elected to the Danish Parliament between 1973-77 and 1979-94, she has also been Chairman of the Danish Parliamentary Committee on Energy, and was Minister for Environment from 1988-90.

Pere Esteve MEP was elected to the European Parliament for the first time in 1999, and sits with the ELDR party. He is a member of Parliament's Committee on Foreign Affairs, Human Rights, Common Security and Defence Policy. Since entering politics by joining Convergencia Democratica de Catalunya (CDC) in 1976, he has been a member of the Catalan Parliament, Secretary General and Spokesman for CDC and List Leader for the CIU in the 1999 European elections.

Dr Werner Hoyer MdB has long been an established member of the ELDR party, culminating in his election as Party President in September 2000. Active within the Free Democratic Party (FDP) since 1972, and a member of the German Bundestag since 1987, he was General Secretary of the FDP between 1993-94. During his time as State Minister for Foreign Affairs from 1994-98, he was one of the architects of the EU's Treaty of Amsterdam.

Anne Jensen MEP is a member of the European Parliament's Committee on Budgets. She began her first term as MEP in 1999 joining the ELDR group. Director for the Danish Federation of Employers from 1994-96, she then took up the post of Chief Editor of the Danish newspaper Berlingske Tidende from 1996-98. She was also Chief Economist in Unibank/Privatbank for the nine years between 1985-94.

Cecilia Malmström MEP is leader of the Swedish Liberal Party in the European Parliament, Folkpartiet liberalerna. She is a member of the ELDR bureau, and sits on Parliament's Committee on Constitutional Affairs. She was elected MEP in 1999, prior to which she was a leading figure in the Liberal EU-referendum campaign in Sweden in 1994, and was a lecturer of Political Science at the University of Goteborg. Since 1998 she has also been a member of the West Swedish Regional Assembly.

Annemie Neyts-Uyttebroeck is the Belgian Minister of State for Foreign Affairs, in charge of agriculture and foreign trade, and, since 1999, has been the President of Liberal International. She was the first (and only) woman to become leader of her party (1985-1989), the Flemish Liberals (VLD). She has served consecutive terms in the House of Representatives and the European Parliament.

Lousewies van der Laan MEP is leader of the Democrats 66 Delegation in the European Parliament and serves as Vice President of Parliament's Committee on Budgetary Control. She also sits on the Committee for Women's Rights and Equal Opportunities. In February 1999 she was elected to head the D66 list at the European elections. Previously, she held a number of posts in the European Commission - in the cabinet of Commissioner van den Broek (1995-97) and as his spokeswoman (1997-99).

Graham Watson MEP is the leader of the UK Liberal Democrats in the European Parliament and Chairman of Parliament's committee on Citizens' Rights and Freedoms, Justice and Home Affairs. Active in Liberal politics since 1972, he has served as general secretary of the international Liberal youth movement and head of the private office to UK Liberal leader Sir David Steel. Works he has previously edited include Liberals in the North-South Dialogue (FNS, 1980) and To the Power of Ten (Centre for Reform, 2000).

Jan-Kees Wiebenga MEP was first elected to the European Parliament in 1994 and is now one of the EP's Vice Presidents. He is also a member of the ELDR bureau, and sits on Parliament's Committee on Citizens' Rights and Freedoms, Justice and Home Affairs. Vice President of the Dutch Liberal Youth Organisation from 1969-71, he then went on to become President of the World Federation of Liberal and Radical Youth. He served in the Dutch Senate and the House of Representatives between 1977-1994.

Introduction

A classical economist's view of economic globalisation might show the world economy as a mathematical equation crossing a vast homogeneous expanse - the earth as a global and virtuous free market ruled by the forces of supply and demand. Trade Ministries in the developed world push in international economic fora, such as the World Trade Organisation, for neo-liberal policies to open national economies to international trade and competition. Meanwhile, the rising anti-globalisation chorus points a critical finger at the same economic policies as an extension of colonial power relations, decrying poverty, environmental degradation and social squalor as a product of globalisation. Developing countries and a vast array of non-governmental organisations, from the World Council of Churches to Friends of the Earth International, call for a re-assessment of current agreements and institutions that promote freer trade.

Liberalism, unsurprisingly, can be found on both sides of the argument. Classical liberalism was founded upon a rejection of theological and mercantile constraints to individual freedom, defining freedom as an absence of constraints imposed by the state and a promotion of laissez-faire economic policies as the path to prosperity. Modern Social Liberalism was born of the recognition that industrialisation had generated new forms of injustice leaving the mass of the population subject to the vagaries of the market. Social Liberalism promotes a positive concept of freedom, maintaining that intervention and aid is needed in an imperfect market place to give disadvantaged individuals the means to fend for themselves.

An ardent free trade advocate today might echo the refrain of a pamphlet of 1840, entitled 'In Defence of Laissez-Faire'[1], which bemoaned the tendency of the public to be "much excited by the tales

---

[1] Source: 'In Defense of Laissez-faire' reprinted in *Battle for the 10-Hour day continues: 4 pamphlets, 1837-1843*, (N.Y.: AMS Press, 1972), pp. 1-8.

11

of hardship" - at that time child labour in British textile factories. However, he or she would be unlikely to be found in today's Liberal parties. Liberalism, as a political movement today, has been more or less influenced by John Stuart Mill, whose autobiography[2] describes his personal journey from classical individualist Liberalism to a Social Liberal awareness of "the deep-rooted selfishness, which forms the general character of the existing state of society".

The viewpoints expressed by the contributors to this book reflect the continuing tensions in Liberal philosophy between its older, classical theorists and the more recent Social Liberal tradition, but their conclusions show a surprising degree of consensus.

John Alderdice considers how growing international co-operation between nations is assisting in conflict resolution. Using the example of Northern Ireland, he identifies how problems which were exacerbated by power imbalance between nation states may be overcome in a supportive broader context, if the ingredients for successful peace negotiations can be found. Central to these, he argues, are the Liberal values of opposition to violence and respect for minority rights. Lone Dybkjær, in a critique of Denmark's attitude to international co-operation, argues that Liberalism's approach to social and political problems will have come of age by 2020, and that the EU will become a global force for Liberalism if Liberals can make it a popular project for the people, rather than a playground for politicians.

Pere Esteve, from a Catalonian perspective, argues that sovereignty and identity are key concepts in a changing world, and that a redistribution of political power is needed. Nothing sustainable can be built if smaller cultures are ignored, he says, and subsidiarity must amount to more than glossy brochures and information offices in major towns. The 'Third Way', which ignores such concepts, cannot provide the answers to globalisation. Werner Hoyer challenges the

---

[2] Source: John Stuart Mill, *Autobiography*, (London, 1873), pp. 230-234.

claims of anti-globalisation protesters that globalisation of the economy is necessarily harmful. On the contrary, he suggests, the social market economy is intrinsically Liberal. Where the protesters have a point is that while the role of the State in a national economy is to provide where the market cannot, no such State exists at the global level. Standards are therefore needed in the form of an Ordnungspolitik, which will allow free market forces to operate within a framework of solidarity.

Similar concerns are expressed by Anne Jensen, who looks at threats to the European Social Model which some perceive comes from globalisation and instead argues that most threats come essentially from within. She uses the Danish textile industry as an example of how success can be found with the right balance between flexibility and security and goes on to argue that market solutions, even in the provision of public services, are not only an effective way forward but are also a democratic instrument of rule, since they reflect the joint outcome of many individual economic choices. Cecilia Malmström believes that the anti-globalisation protesters are often Liberals who have been misled. Explaining why the Tobin tax could not work, she calls for a new emphasis on the old Liberal ideas of open markets, free trade, free movement of people and international solidarity, concluding that closed borders have never been a sound policy for freedom and prosperity and that only genuine global free trade will lead to freer societies.

Annemie Neyts-Uyttebroeck also believes that Liberals must provide intelligent answers to the critics of globalisation. The case for universalism is a Liberal case, she says, because the individual freedom in which only Liberals believe, including gender equality, is a precondition for successful economic development. Lousewies van der Laan distinguishes between Social Liberalism and economic Liberalism, arguing that the former is the real guardian of democratic control and public accountability. Power is too distant, she says, and corrupts those possessing it. The challenge to Liberals is to promote international co-operation, regionally and globally, while respecting democracy.

Graham Watson, inspired by the belief that human values are essentially the same in every community, concludes that the challenges to humankind require a new emphasis on and new approaches to global governance and that the management structures of our world must evolve to take account of this. He foresees the development of a world parliament to hold to account those responsible for decisions taken globally. Jan-Kees Wiebenga believes that the impact of globalisation is currently greater in its immaterial parameters, such as the spread of democracy, human rights and the rule of law than in the economic field. Globalisation forces a confrontation between western Liberal ideals and other ideologies and provides a framework for dialogue with countries such as the People's Republic of China, which would enhance human freedom. While the EU needs reform, it is nonetheless a bright star in a sometimes dark sky, he maintains, and a model of governance worthy of export.

While each of the contributors favours free trade, none believes it to be organised at present in a sustainable, just or democratic framework. Economic, social and political inequalities demand more than trite sloganeering, whether it is by globalisation's loudest apostles or its fiercest opponents. Ill-considered simplification or deliberate misrepresentation of the challenges of globalisation will leave the guilty looking shabby in the history books. The promotion of a free trade agenda does not conflict with addressing the concerns of the Social Liberal tradition, but nor can any politician seriously maintain that unfettered market forces are a panacea for all ills. The test for Liberals is the search for balance.

Liberalism offers a fascinating tradition for politicians and others to mine for answers to the questions posed by the debate over globalisation. Liberals must avoid triumphalism at the current neo-liberal consensus, recognising where freer trade and social welfare policies perpetuate existing problems and seeking to reconcile the best of the economic Liberal and Social Liberal approaches. The anti-globalisation demonstrations, attended by many thousands of people in Gothenburg and Genoa this year, do not represent a mass political or cultural tide of change in public opinion, yet. The consensus over economic matters in financial journals may insist that the neo-liberal agenda must prevail, yet even the WTO now admits to a need to engage with its critics. Failure to address these issues, however, and the problems highlighted by the critics of globalisation in an honest and undogmatic fashion will make the responsible politician a byword to future generations, a byword for arrogance and complacency.

Graham Watson MEP
Howard Mollett

September 2001

Liberalism and Conflict Resolution

John Alderdice

Globalisation is most frequently talked about in terms of economics, so it is not surprising that agreements reached in the World Trade Organisation and the sometimes violent protests against G8 economic summits provide most of the column inches that reflect on the 'globalisation' phenomenon. At the European level, outside of Northern Ireland, the Balkans and perhaps Cyprus, the advent of the euro is currently foremost in the minds of most of our fellow citizens.

The prominence of economics in the euro debate is attributable not only to the historical and emotional enormity of this step away from nation statism, but also because it directly affects our daily lives and the money in our pockets. Unsurprisingly, the Liberals, particularly in Britain, have been more clear and forceful in their advocacy of the single currency than the other political families, for it represents in a simple but substantial way the freedom to travel and to trade, for which Liberals have long worked and argued. These freedoms are not just ends in themselves but are essential to combat Beveridge's five giants of Want, Squalor, Disease, Ignorance and Idleness. Measured against such markers, the European Union is already an extraordinary economic and social success. That is why so many other European countries are desperate to join the single market and share in its prosperity.

In this focus on economic cooperation, it is often forgotten that for the original architects of 'ever closer union' the driving force was not primarily a commitment to economic liberalism, but a reaction to their experience of the horrors of war. Europe had many wars throughout the centuries and the humiliation and misery of conflict had been the common experience of almost every generation, but the repeated and unprecedented destruction of two World Wars demonstrated that nationalism and imperialism offered no stability to the people of Europe. Worse still, scientific advance had created the frightening prospect that a future war would be even more catastrophic.

In the 19th Century, two conflicting strands of thinking had developed in British Liberalism. The love of liberty led some to support actively those who were fighting for independence and freedom from despotism, while the love of peace led other Liberals to advocate non-intervention. The first half of the 20th Century showed that so long as the relations between peoples are governed by independent states seeking only their own short-term interests, both of these approaches tend to lead to war, not freedom or peace. This was a profound challenge to Liberalism. The 19th Century had been driven by optimism that education and scientific advancement would build a new, free and civilized world. Science, art, culture, sociology and the study of the mind all indicated that things were evolving for the better, but as the deluge which swamped the world in 1914 subsided four years later, that optimism had been swept away.

Things were indeed changing and progress was being made, but was it certain that it was all for the better? Conservatives thought not, but could only rail impotently against the tides of history. Liberals hoped that the end of empires and the extension of the suffrage would lead independent people and states to build a new world at peace with itself. It was not to be. The League of Nations was insufficient in its task, and the advancements of science brought an increased opportunity for destruction too. Progressive thinking seemed to slip towards Socialism with its trust in the masses, qualified, not as Gladstone's trust had been by prudence, but by political dogma. Socialism also had an unqualified and unjustified belief that science would answer the dilemmas of the human condition.

Previously, the slowness of communication and travel and the power of physical force and traditional explosives had limited the capacity for destruction through war. Radio, air travel and nuclear power changed all that. The beneficial opportunities for wealth creation and distribution were dazzling, but to the silver lining there was a dark cloud. The speed of change ensured that not only could things get better more quickly, they could also deteriorate with great speed. The Second World War ended with the demonstration that man at war could lose all the vestiges of civilization in the holocaust, and could now with certainty destroy his enemy and all life on the planet. Men no longer went off to war. War now visited itself, with terrifying results on whole communities through air bombardment.

The boundaries had gone and it changed completely and irrevocably the significance of conflict. Any local war could now escalate into global destruction. Independence was not a solution but an illusion. Liberal thinkers moved beyond placing their hope in the independence of nation states to interdependence through international cooperation. This was the basis for the United Nations and for the rapid development of international law. It was also the context for a remarkable experiment in international liberal democracy in Europe. Its purpose was to ensure freedom from war.

In Europe, which had been the cockpit of the conflicts, the fear of war was greatest. To the traditional rivalries between France, Britain and Germany was added the now more terrifying prospect of being the turf upon which a nuclear conflict would be fought out between the USSR and the USA. War was now too terrible to contemplate and was to be prevented at all costs. Cooperation on the economic reconstruction of a devastated Europe opened the route to new models of cross-border cooperation, and the pooling of sovereignty in an increasing range of competencies. Fifty years later, war between historic Western European rivals like Germany and France is unthinkable and the success of the process continues to manifest itself in the resolution of long-standing, albeit smaller scale conflicts, such as that in Northern Ireland. It may be useful to examine the Irish Peace Process in this light because while violent conflict between the major European states is now only a remote possibility, there remain, in places like Cyprus and the Balkans, ancient feuds, which remain unresolved and dangerous.

When the civil rights marches in Northern Ireland in 1968 broke down into serious civil unrest, the first reaction of the Government was to deal with the problem as a matter of internal security. Even nationalist leaders at the time presented their case as one of fighting for British rights for British citizens. It became obvious at an early stage, however, that while the setting for the trouble was within Northern Ireland, the context was the still unresolved relationship between Britain and Ireland. Britain had hoped the matter had been laid to rest by the settlement in 1922, when the island partitioned, and had treated Northern Ireland less as an integral part of the United Kingdom, and more as a self-governing dominion. The South meanwhile emphasized and developed its independence by leaving the British Commonwealth, becoming a Republic, remaining neutral during the Second World War and refusing to join the NATO military alliance.

The period from 1923 to 1968 saw only sporadic terrorist activity so there was no real threat to stability, and neither government paid much attention to the dormant problem. As elsewhere, independence of operation was the leitmotif of this period. More liberal and tolerant societies in the North and South might have mitigated the smouldering hatreds and perhaps even prevented the subsequent Troubles. Much could have been done by way of appreciation of the educational, cultural and social needs of the Catholic minority in the North and the Protestant minority in the South. Cross-border economic cooperation would have made a substantial difference to relations. Instead, Eamon de Valera developed the South as an avowedly Catholic Nationalist state with an antipathy to all things British, and the North was governed in the interests of the Protestant majority.

After fifty years of partition, the results were predictable. Few Protestants remained in the southern state and the substantial Catholic minority in the North felt isolated, alienated and resentful. Neither part of the island was economically successful. Breakdown was inevitable and when it came it was very bloody. Three thousand were killed and tens of thousands injured in the years of violence that followed. The internal government was prorogued in 1972 and the

Protestant/Catholic power-sharing arrangement that followed it collapsed after only six months of operation in 1974. It all seemed very hopeless.

By a fortunate turn of history, the United Kingdom and the Republic of Ireland joined the European Economic Community in 1973. As a result, government ministers, political leaders and other opinion formers found themselves meeting regularly with each other as member states in a new cooperative venture. The structure of the Common Market recognized that the United Kingdom was larger, but still treated the Republic of Ireland as an equal member. This changed the context of Anglo-Irish relations. Gradually mutual respect grew as practical working arrangements developed, and by 1985 an Anglo-Irish Agreement was signed laying the foundations for unprecedented cooperation in addressing the Northern Ireland issue. Separate development was giving way to working together.

There is an important general principle here. It is unremarkable to observe that many long-standing disputes arise at the boundaries between, or more correctly, just inside the borders of sovereign states, and are symptomatic of unresolved relationships between them. In the past this tended to lead to wars between states. Now the consequences of such conflagrations are so serious that intra state conflicts are much more common. This can obscure the fact that the violence is not just a result of local difficulties within the state borders but is symptomatic of problems between larger powers. The situation in Cyprus, for example, cannot properly be understood unless it is viewed in the broader context of Greek-Turkish relations, and it is hard to see how the problems of that divided island can be resolved without addressing these larger questions. If the dynamic of European Union enlargement can be harnessed there, as it was for the Northern Ireland conflict, the prospects for progress may be enhanced.

The 1985 Anglo-Irish Agreement improved relations between Britain and Ireland, but did not of itself resolve the conflict in Northern Ireland. While Catholic Nationalists felt less isolated, the Irish Republican Army (IRA) continued its terrorist campaign in the hope of furthering their aims. Unionists meantime felt betrayed by Britain and Protestant paramilitaries took revenge through further sectarian killings. It took six years of diplomatic activity to get political representatives of the two sides in Northern Ireland even to sit around a table to talk. This emphasizes the other side of the coin. While it is impossible to solve such problems without addressing the external relationships between the major regional powers, they also cannot be resolved without the people themselves playing their part. This is often misunderstood by those who view politics as merely the balance between the major international military and economic powers and how they choose to exercise control. Liberals maintain that the people of the regions and local communities cannot be forced to solve conflicts. They must be involved through their own representatives. This is not just true in the resolution of violent conflicts, it is also true in maintaining the integrity of democratic politics in any circumstances. Referendums have shown more than once how even the European Union risks losing the support of its citizens when it becomes centralized in its decision-making or dominated by the large members.

The wider international community is of course important and the Northern Ireland Peace Process required the involvement of the EU and the United States of America, particularly during the two Clinton administrations. There were at least two key roles: providing economic assistance, and bringing encouragement and mediation. Such external intervention is common in communities in crisis, but the approach to both of these roles may vary widely.

A liberal economic agenda tends to concentrate its economic assistance less on grants and more on assisting with sustainable economic development. The International Fund for Ireland was established to channel much of the financial aid from the USA, the EU, Canada, Australia and New Zealand and it has targeted its aid in precisely this way. There was training, consultancy and advice for small businesses and community groups which were trying to build a more entrepreneurial economy. This was especially important where the community had become dependent on a high level of British

Treasury subvention. The main emphasis has been to help people build their own wealth, take control of their own affairs, and increase their engagement in commerce and trade with the outside world.

The approach of Senator George Mitchell, as chairman of the multi-party talks that led eventually to the Belfast Agreement in 1998, was also Liberal in its character. He did not bring his own solutions to the talks. He listened patiently and carefully for a very long time to all the different parties to the problem, excluded no one, and created a process where the parties brought their proposals to him in the presence of each other. Of course they did not reach agreement in this way, but he built such trust that when the parties had exhausted the process of talking, they asked him to bring forward proposals. In the book he wrote detailing his work in Northern Ireland he describes how the whole process almost collapsed when the British and Irish Governments, impatient at the slow pace, took control themselves and tried to impose their own views. This work of building a process, rather than conjuring up a solution, is the heart of conflict resolution. It requires skill and stamina and may take many years, and it can only bring success when carried out in a supportive broader context. If the external powers continue their disputes vicariously through the regional conflict, all attempts at resolution are doomed to fail.

The experience of the European Union also showed itself in the content of the Belfast Agreement. The cross-border cooperation, so foundational in the EU and largely absent in Ireland for over fifty years, was the model for the North-South Ministerial Council. This institution brings together, in summit and in sectoral format, ministers from the devolved government in Northern Ireland and the sovereign government in the Republic of Ireland to deal with areas of shared concern, including agriculture, economic development, environmental protection and transport. The variable geometry of the British-Irish Council brings together not only ministers from London and Dublin, but also the devolved administrations in Edinburgh, Cardiff and Belfast, as well as the Isle of Man and the Channel Islands. It is difficult to see how an imperial Britain or a newly independent Ireland could have contemplated such a model without the example and the years of experience of a European Union that gives equal esteem (though not of course equal representation) to, for example, Germany and Luxembourg.

These five components - the critical part played by influential *external relationships*, the difficult but necessary *inclusion of the representatives of all local parties*, the creation of *sustainable economic development and cross-border trade*, patient and skilful mediation through a *long-term talks process*, and *institutional creativity* - are all vital aspects of conflict resolution and key characteristics of the European Union. They are necessary ingredients, but they are not sufficient for success. There are at least two others.

Liberals are not by temperament warmongers. They accept the use of force only in extremis, and as a result tend to be more imaginative in devising alternatives to violence. This is not always a majority position. Demagogues can often raise enthusiastic support for the proposition that war is preferable to cooperation with others, and the history of Europe is littered with examples. The European Union would not have developed as it has had not the people, and political leaders of France, Germany, Italy and the Benelux come through tragic and overwhelming experience to regard war with rank horror. Until people in any conflict begin to turn away from violence as a means of solving their predicament, they are unlikely to be prepared to accept that the prize of peace is worth the price of peace.

The final element is the most difficult of all, and it involves the protection of minorities. There are many aspects to this issue but it is of primary importance, indeed it is the problem that lies at the core of many conflicts. The classic liberal commitment to freedom under the rule of law creates an environment for the protection of minorities, and the developing corpus of human rights practice provides a framework by which the protection of individuals and groups may be measured and ensured. These international legal norms and structures are in themselves rarely a sufficient guarantor for the partisans in a conflict. Usually political vetoes are required. In the European Union, this took the form of the requirement for unanimity in decisions at the Council of Ministers. In the Dayton Agreement, the three warring factions, Serb, Croat and Bosnian all had their own separate parties, and nothing could be agreed without three-way assent. In Northern Ireland, the formation of the Assembly is precisely proportionate to the percentage vote, for numbers of seats, membership and chairmanship of committees and even for ministerial positions. This guarantees both sections of the community positions in government at all times. The mutual veto was then taken further with a requirement that the First and Deputy First Ministers be a partnership elected on a single slate by a majority of unionists and a majority of nationalists. These joint office bearers stand or fall together and can only make decisions jointly.

While it is clear that this tight model of power-sharing guarantees minority involvement, it is not difficult to see how such a settlement could hold the seeds of its own destruction, for there is something a little illiberal about it. The liberal concern for cooperation and mutuality is satisfied. The liberal requirement for liberty and flexibility is less fulfilled. The problem is not just the lack of liberty, but knowledge of human nature would tell us that the very sense of compulsion inherent in the model may, in the future, provoke the very rebellion it is designed to suppress. The strain on this rigid form of protection is an issue in the European Union where there is increasing pressure to accept qualified majority on a wider range of issues. The dilemma is clear. Whether to trust the majority to respect the needs and wishes of the smaller countries, or whether to depend on maintaining a unanimity requirement and risk stagnation, gridlock and eventually a collapse of the whole edifice.

Here we move beyond formulae and regulations in preventing and resolving conflict. What Liberals understand is that while relationships cannot survive without the stability of boundaries, they are based on more than the observance of rules. There must also be a spirit of generosity and respect. Without this they cannot flourish and conflict is never truly put to the past. Rules can provide the context for a conflict to be stopped, but only a new culture of mutual respect can prevent it returning. An enlarging European Union will falter and choke if it depends on ever more complex and restrictive rules. Developing that political culture of respect and trust is the task that this generation cannot delegate to the next; either in Northern Ireland, or in the widening European Union.

I have concentrated in this chapter on the examples of Europe and Northern Ireland, but the purpose has been to draw out principles that are relevant to concepts of conflict resolution in an increasingly interdependent, increasingly globalised world. The forces that have changed the picture in these examples are also showing themselves in some measure everywhere else. That is why regional networks and institutions are making their appearance in the Americas and in Asia. It is also the case that some elements and participants in the Northern Ireland Peace Process came from other parts of the world, for example, South Africa. That said, we in Europe gave the rest of the world two terrible wars. It is our reparative challenge to be an exemplar of interdependence for a world that has few more attractive options.

On Being a Liberal in 2020

Lone Dybkjær

Dear Patrick, relatives and friends.

First and foremost, congratulations on your 19th birthday. What an idea for a birthday speech! 'How Denmark looked in the year you were born', back in the beginning of the third millennium. And all of this before dinner! Let this toast offer us some food for thought.

The Danish political system is characterized by its many political parties and minority governments to the extent that the last majority government from 1993-1994 was actually accused of being undemocratic. Minority governments are forced to submit proposals for major compromises in order to secure a majority. The tough negotiations that result from this process are both positive and negative, as it becomes increasingly difficult to differentiate between the various governments.

My party, Det Radikale Venstre, the Danish Social Liberal Party, was formed in 1905 as a breakaway party from Venstre, the Liberal Party. We have always sought influence and have often been in government, mostly with Socialdemokratiet, the Social Democratic Party, but also with the Liberal Party and Det Konservative Folkeparti, the Conservative People's Party.

Denmark was perfect neither then nor now. Still, I remember how happy I was that you were born here. We can never know what life brings, so it is a blessing to have the security of being born in a country with a strong sense of security developed through shared responsibility. We cannot eliminate misfortunes and pain, but we can relieve them. We cannot eliminate inequalities, but we can reduce them. It was these ideals which lay behind models such as the Scandinavian Welfare Model.

But it was exactly this model that was challenged during the years after you were born. Challenges and the necessary changes came about due to new conditions, new technology and new demands from the citizens, not least due to population changes. The Danish Welfare Model was based on a homogenous population with a shared cultural background. This pattern was broken when, in the last part of the 20th Century, just as Europe's population aged, countries also opened economic and physical borders, becoming heavily dependent on a global trading system that challenged the boundaries of the nation state.

Denmark has always been an open society dependent to a large degree on foreign trade, but always within the context of the relatively closed borders of the traditional nation state. Globalisation changed this context and this was of course emphasised through our involvement in EU co-operation. Globalisation was at that time still not perceived by the broader public as the most obvious problem, despite a vigorous debate among economic powers and the politically engaged, from environmental activists to Chief Executives in transnational corporations.

Instead, migrant workers and our participation in the EU unfortunately became scapegoat issues in the debate about many of the difficult economic and political re-adjustments to the opening-up brought about by the many effects of globalisation. We concentrated on those people of non-Danish origin as Denmark had failed to handle immigration in a fair and comprehensive manner. A number of population groups were poorly integrated in Danish society and immigrants had an unemployment rate three and a half times higher than the rest of the population. The right wing political debate focused on a polarised racist discourse and a misrepresentation of the facts, exacerbating the problems of integration. These controversies overshadowed a sensible and necessary debate on the reorganisation of Danish society in light of the new challenges and opportunities.

In this period, the Social Democratic - Social Liberal government often used the term 'Denmark as a pioneer' and after some time, I came to feel that the expression was a double-edged sword. In many respects, Denmark had been justly celebrated for progressive attitudes and policies regarding areas such as fighting poverty, creating equal opportunities for both sexes and so on. And yet, perhaps for this very reason, it had also resulted in a self-perception among the Danish population that anything Danish was good, and everything else was not. This was particularly evident in the debate about the European Union. After failing initially to recognise public misgivings about immigration, welfare reform, the EU and other globalisation issues, the Danish Social Liberal Party realised that it would need eventually to pioneer a public debate, challenging constructively the divisive and negative frame of mind that saw only black and white. Raising the issues with a public alienated from the international institutions and the political structures driving the processes became the challenge for the 21st Century.

We succeeded, handling immigration in our own Danish way by accepting finally that it was an issue of class division, an unknown phenomenon in Denmark at that time. This was established along our own Danish model: a combination of "rights and duties". Today, we are yet again a society that functions on a strong Social Liberal foundation; senstivity, ideas, pragmatism, visions and political craftsmanship at it's best.

At the same time we handled the debate about the EU which proved to be frustrating, since even I did not view the contemporary European Union's institutions and decision-making procedures as a perfect system in any way. On the contrary, there was so much to change, which by all means demanded energy, but not the kind of misrepresentative and ignorant debate promulgated by the EU opponents in Denmark. There were five points that constituted the essential issues to be addressed for countering this misguided debate in Denmark and to promote a measured perspective on the European Union.

Firstly, I felt that the opponents denied the historical aspect of the Second World War: that the EU was originally formed to prevent a new war. This may have seemed absurd at the turn of the new millennium, but it proved that the project had been successful. The 20th Century's onslaught in terms of the unprecedented wars and violations of human rights was all the more reason to find hope within the well functioning institutions of democracies as found within EU borders. Through peaceful co-operation, conflicts could be solved by words and not weapons, or in some cases (for example in Northern Ireland and the Basque region) at least contained.

Secondly, the opponents denied the economic opportunities that had been afforded by the EU. Agriculture agreements within the EU meant that up to the year 2000, Denmark was a net beneficiary rather than a net contributor to European co-operation. All Danish businesses had benefited from the European market. Money is not everything, but no one can tell me that it is unimportant.

The third issue at the time was the effective denial of globalisation. Critics argued in favour of a simplistic return to 'the way things were', rather than confronting the political imperatives of an ever-more globalised world in terms of the new formations in economics, communications, as well as the rising environmental and social challenges. All these changes for both the better and the worse demanded energy and commitment in facing the challenges of globalisation, rather than retreating from them.

The fourth was our opponents' vision of international co-operation between equal states. A fine vision, unfortunately just not of this world. People may be equal but nations are not. Europe is not composed of 80 states the size of Denmark. Germany, France and Britain are powerful on the European scene because of their size and the EU project is necessary to ensure political and economic co-operation instead of pure domination.

But, for me, the fifth reason was the most fundamental and probably the issue that affected me the most. Namely, the type of debate carried out by EU opponents in Denmark, which constituted nothing less than an indirect denial of the ground rules of democracy. The Danish EU opponents did not want to participate in Danish decisions about the EU in the Danish parliament, nor did they promote a sophisticated and democratic public debate in Denmark. That they chose merely to speak out against everything in the European Parliament, raising the issue simply in a one-dimensional sloganeering fashion in Denmark at European Parliament elections, this upset me.

It seemed necessary to renew the very course of democracy in Denmark in the wake of this disheartening spectacle. The European Union itself provides an example of intergovernmental co-operation in all these very different fields, from environmental protection and redistributive funding for deprived regions to regulation of financial markets and common external trade policies, striking a balance between the demands of its social and economic pillars.

Indeed, the European Union had the potential and sometimes managed to live up to its claim to be a 'global player'. The EU has shown itself to offer a necessary counter-weight to those proponents of an economic globalisation driven exclusively by the concerns of rich developed world countries in the North and transnational corporations. In international negotiations on topics as diverse as climate change or reform of offshore banking, the EU acted as a global Liberal conscience. These examples underline how the denial of globalisation was clearly a self-defeating argument. In this respect, the European Union became a global force for Social Liberal values.

This, however, was not treated as a core issue, either by those engaged in public debate, or by leaders in the European Parliament. Instead, the discussion was too caught up in arcane institutional questions and the belief that a simple re-weighting of power in Parliament's favour would suffice. A reorientation of the discussion towards issues that were important to the population was required to make the European Union a profitable and popular project for its citizens, more than just a playground for politicians.

At the time, the EU was not a popular project. In Denmark, this was evident in two lost referendums. Fortunately, at the turn of the new millennium, we succeeded in initiating a new discussion, this time about the ratification of the Nice Treaty. It produced, however, a result with which many in the European Parliament were dissatisfied and which an increasing number of people thought an awkward process as negotiations had taken between four and five days. But, is it so strange that it takes time for 15 countries to agree on rather extensive reforms, especially when there are great disparities between the countries' economic and power related interests?

As a Danish writer and essayist commented:

"Democracy is the work of man and only the work of man. But it is the first form of government the populations wish to live under, and which is consistently founded on peace between political adversaries in a state. As a result, the state's legitimacy draws on a certain practised moral in the power struggle, though not in the state's relationship with other states. International law has not yet become the constitution for states' mutual interaction that it dreamed it would be but if it is ever to become so, it is obvious that only democratic power control in states can constitute the foundation for corresponding control between them."[3]

Opponents to 'globalisation' per se do themselves no favours, essentially confusing a whole mass of different political, economic, social and cultural developments that are reduced to a simplistic narrative that fits only certain ideological viewpoints. Seeing only black and white, the anti-globalisation movements too often denied the political and economic emancipatory opportunities offered by a globalised political consciousness amongst the public and practical political co-operation at the international level. These measures, whether newly established instruments and institutions, sanctions or regulations are sometimes flawed but all offer an improvement on going it alone at the national level.

---

[3] Ulrich Horst Petersen, *The Time of Trial – Essays 1997-2000*, Gyldendal, 2001.

Social Liberalism has proved to be the political philosophy for the 21st Century precisely because it did not cling to the extreme ideological 'eternal verities' of left and right, but sought the framework to make its core humanistic values work.

The Danish Social Liberal Party managed to develop and renew itself, emphasising core values such as the right to personal development and a corresponding solidarity at national and global social levels. It is in the tension between reality and vision that politics moves!

A toast to Patrick on his 19th birthday! Unfortunately, the political history and ideals I have described could never hope to satisfy a nineteen year old. I hope that you and your generation can succeed in putting more of such idealism into the next twenty years of history and beyond!

National Identity, Globalisation and Democracy from a Catalan Perspective

Pere Esteve

On Liberalism

Europe seems to be leaning towards and tempted by the so-called 'Third Way', from the British New Labour Party to the Spanish Partido Popular (The People's Party). It is effectively a search for the political centre. In order to achieve this, a fusion between both traditional right and left wing programmes is needed. This phenomenon is also the reflection of a certain weariness felt by citizens towards both politics and politicians, and the retreat of politics into a style that an Economist review described as "awesomely, magisterially, and in some ways disturbingly, vacuous"[4].

In the changes brought about by globalisation (especially in the fields of information, culture and economics), causes and consequences are often hard to distinguish, but it is clear that, as usual, the world of politics lags behind such changes. The main virtue of the Third Way is that it has detected a trend: the blurring of ideological extremes and a drift towards the centre. Naturally, these changes and how they are felt differ from country to country. The sustainability of the Third Way will depend on whether it is approached out of necessity, or arrived at for reasons of party advantage.

In this context, I would like to reflect on why Liberalism, conceived of by some as a Third Way, is unable to enjoy the apparent success of Third Way politics all over the European continent. In what respect can Liberals offer a vision of their own for the future?

---

[4] The Economist, review of Anthony Giddens, *The Third Way*, 19 September 1998.

I believe it is necessary for Liberals now to begin a new phase of reflection and action. Despite the triumphalism of the Third Way, it would be a mistake to adopt a tone of "we told you so" or claim that "we are the genuine Third Way". Two points need to be stressed. First of all, it is necessary to assume a critical, and in some sense etymological, awareness of the concept of "the Third Way". Secondly, it is important to expose the deceptive quality of some of its assumptions, particularly to reveal proposals and actions that move away from the centre, for the Orwellian trumpeting of Third Way as "non-ideological" or "beyond the ideological" is clearly nonsense. One thinks, for instance, of the debate over whether to promote private involvement in the provision of public services. Moving towards mixed provision does nothing to resolve ideological differences.

The consequences of globalisation are so new that Liberals must elaborate concrete proposals to address the many political and economic challenges at the threshold of the 21st Century, for instance with regard to development and reform of the European Union. How can we incorporate recent innovations into the old Liberal ideals? How can we assure greater freedom in the 21st Century? How can greater social justice be achieved? How should the market place be organised? How should we organise ourselves, both socially and politically? How should power be distributed? All these questions now require new answers appropriate to a globalised world.

In this instance, my contribution is formed by reflecting on a nation: Catalonia. Catalonia has a long history and today, its size and demography matches that of several member states of the European Union, yet it is still not internationally recognised. To this day, Catalonia, like so many of the smaller member states and many of the regions, is permitted no genuine and direct political participation in the European Union's institutions and political processes. In the light of this, it is natural to include reflections on my nation, whose people are the object and driving force of my own political work.

Reflecting on the democratic deficit evident in such international and regional formations as the European Union, (i.e. institutions of the new globalising order), will necessarily touch on concepts such as subsidiarity but also, simultaneously, on our own image. Concepts of a national identity and the nationalist image must be reviewed and updated.

In the new era, understanding national identities and drawing out their universal traits might be one of the keys to a better understanding of our present situation and a clearer view of the challenges of globalisation. I believe that the example of Catalonia has much to offer on this point. Nationalism in Catalonia is built around long term and historically founded concepts of social integration, co-existence, respect for others and a sense of solidarity. The cohesion of Catalan society is both the result of forces intrinsic to a defined social and culture identity, a national 'Catalan identity', and of the will of individuals to share the building of a common future. The challenge of promoting integration and solidarity in a globalising world is to make the human ties and the human aspects of these processes apparent, to prevent alienation and promote participation in expanding regional and global level politics. Thus, a re-distribution of political power in Europe (as well as major institutional reform) is one of the most important steps in assuring the democratic legitimacy of the EU, a challenge reflected in every globalisation process.

Furthermore, the complex traits associated with the evolution of national identities and their recognition of the new regional and global political configurations also underline the point that the complex realities of present day Europe cannot be interpreted solely on the basis of the right / left axis. The great Liberal challenge is to become the protagonists of a new era.

Catalonia and emerging ideas in Europe

European member states and the nations contained within them are experiencing a slow and self-evident transformation resulting from two major forces acting on the nation state: an inner force and an outer force.

Firstly, states are increasingly dependent on structures that from a technological, military, cultural or economic point of view are vast and overpowering. The State has lost much control over its own economy, particularly as a result of the continuing liberalisation reform processes and the Economic and Monetary Union project of the European Union. With regards to security and defence, nation state strategies appear to be obsolete in Europe.

States are obliged to yield political power. At the top, the most pressing issues are those negotiated at supranational and intergovernmental level, affecting the shared security and common interests of the European Union member states: issues such as justice, defence, international politics and the economic restrictions which affect them. Within the increasingly interdependent European Union, it is joint action decided at EU level that provides for defence, security and economic development. We all feel safe within the European Union and with the support of the Allies. Europe gives us peace of mind.

At the grassroots level are issues related to identity, culture, education and social services. In other words, issues related to oneself and to the creation of areas for social interaction which are easy to access and which are closer to home and easier to influence.

It was Bob Dylan who sang, "the times they are a-changing." And, indeed, they are changing, at least in Europe, with respect to two key issues - sovereignty (political power and the division of that power between national and EU level decision-making) and identity. In a recent book, Alain Touraine posed the question, "Is there anybody who seriously believes that an entire society can be governed by a centralised system?" I believe the answer to be, obviously, no.

The changes outlined above point to a significant transformation in the traditional forms of political action. They point towards a new cultural policy for an old continent, a new political culture that is emerging in Europe and that is gathering momentum as a result of the economic and social changes brought about due to economic globalisation. Such changes should tend towards a decentralisation of power, and yet it is this project that is far from fruition. The political stimulus provided by the European Union to preserve the diversity of languages and cultures must be increased to ensure the democratic legitimacy of the whole project. Subsidiarity, as currently practiced, is an ill-defined concept. Public participation must amount to more than glossy brochures and a few information offices in major towns across the continent.

In Catalonia, the ingredients for such a new political culture are already present. As a nation we have demonstrated that we are capable of creating the conditions for real change. In this new political culture we do not want simply to be understood, or tolerated, but rather to play an active role. The EU must open up to the demands of its under-represented and insufficiently consulted regions, nations and citizens to identify the real problems which are not recognised in the grand visions for the EU outlined by heads of state, or in the current theoretical or actual political structures. An inclusive dynamism must be the objective. It is time to open up rather than to close up. For Catalonia, as for so many other nations awaiting participation in the new global political institutions, many political products have expiry dates that have come and gone.

In the European Union, as in other political and economic formations of the 21st Century, nothing sustainable can be built if smaller, less powerful, nations and their different identities and cultures are ignored. Politics must be built with one's mind as well as one's heart. Along this road, Europe is looking for models, signposts, beacons. If Europe is looking for references, then I can only stress that Catalonia offers one response to this need. There are many others.

Catalonia is a singular example of how, throughout history, a group of people has been able to preserve cohesion and identity. They have achieved this without ever having the structure of a state and above all, preferring freedom and the rights of individuals to everything else. The European Union will suffer in the long term if it fails to recognise the importance of such foundational necessities as the power of national and group identities: social and cultural belonging that must be given political expression and power. A failure to ensure democratic legitimacy for the European Union may not be an immediate issue for those caught up in the details of legislation in this or that field, but will be decisive in determining the sustainability of the project as a whole.

Globalisation, Social Market Economies and Development

Werner Hoyer[5]

The violent protests and mass public movement against globalisation which accompanied the sessions of the World Trade Organisation in Seattle, the World Economic Forum in Davos, the Summit of the Americas in Quebec and the G8 in Genoa, seemed to imply both that globalisation is something immoral and that it can be averted. This is a double misunderstanding.

Firstly, there is no alternative to globalisation. It is happening whether we want it or not. Whilst theoretically, trade liberalisation could be reversed by raising trade barriers and re-introducing capital controls, in reality the integration of markets has progressed so far that such action would have immediate negative effects on the economy. Multinational companies would not be the only ones to resist strongly such an attempt to roll back economic integration. Furthermore, technological progress, especially in the fields of information and communication, is one of the key driving forces of economic globalisation and is irreversible. Therefore, fighting against globalisation is, to put it in economic terms, a waste of resources.

Secondly, and more importantly, while it can be questioned whether or not the concepts of morality or immorality may be applied to the process of globalisation as such, the perception of globalisation as generally detrimental is also erroneous. Globalisation does not lead to mass unemployment or to concern solely for "shareholder value" in industrialised countries, nor does it necessarily increase poverty in developing countries, and it does not render national governments powerless or economic policy redundant. To state that there are few

---

[5] I would like to thank Hans Carl von Werthern for his help and contributions in writing this chapter.

winners and numerous losers of globalisation is inaccurate and unfair. On the contrary, in the longer term, the overall effects of globalisation will prove beneficial for the welfare of the whole world. There are, however, some preconditions.

Our belief in the beneficial effects of globalisation is based on the model of a social market economy at the national level, an intrinsically Liberal concept. Liberal economic thinking holds that the market is the best way of allocating resources. According to this Liberal view, the market mechanism redirects the individual's striving for profit into satisfying the (economic) needs of society. Therefore, Liberalism wants to free market forces for the benefit of all.

The market should be allowed to function as freely as possible. Direct state interventions should be reduced to a minimum whilst providing for checks and balances to unfettered market power. A combination of the failure of ambitious economic intervention and the unpopularity of high taxation has made governments recognise that cutting taxes and public spending, de-regulating and privatising are the most promising ways to raise productivity and the standard of living. This also works on an international or global level. Globalisation hence implies the opportunity to increase productivity, growth and welfare by increasing international trade and the division of labour.

Liberal economic theorists provide the orientation for the multilateral trading system - they map the future of a globalised world economy. A long and illustrious tradition, going back to Ricardo and Adam Smith, has shown how two countries can obtain mutual gains from trade, both specialising in the sectors that constitute their comparative advantage, both profiting from the efficiency gains of a shared trading system as a guard against the insecurities of protectionism.

In other words, trade raises the welfare of all partners involved, including those who have less favourable conditions of production in all fields. If the markets are allowed to function, trade will develop to this effect, precisely because all of the trading partners are striving to maximise their profits. Very possibly, it is especially the 'weaker' partners who gain most from this exchange. For this reason, free trade has become accepted as the driving economic agenda all over the world.

The ideas of free trade economics are still not fully backed by a majority of our populations or governments. Profit, and therefore the market economy, are widely considered to be morally impaired. Governments are apologising for globalisation and promising to civilise it, instead of explaining its potential to the public. However, confronting the anti-globalisation movement requires that the intelligent commentator also confronts the fact that globalisation is not without risks. The present speed of globalisation risks over-exerting the adaptability of nations and societies. At the time of writing, the European Union and the United States of America seek to persuade developing countries to sign up to a new round of trade liberalisation measures at the World Trade Organisation (WTO) Ministerial meeting in Qatar in November 2001. These efforts continue despite the repeated assertions by the developing world that it is simply not ready for more issues to be brought under the WTO regime, and that questions of implementation of the current commitments must be addressed first. Moreover, the financial crises of the last decade, especially those in Latin America and in Asia, were triggered by excessive volatility in the flow of capital which amplified the negative effects of unsustainable budgetary policies in these regions.

The central problem, however, is the fact that too many people have been excluded from the benefits of globalisation. The protesters are right in pointing out, and Liberals share the view, that the most pressing moral, political and economic issues of today are Third World poverty. But, this is not a consequence of globalisation itself. It is rather a result of the fact that globalisation is not truly global enough yet. If developing countries were in a position to participate in the global markets, the world's poor would profit from productive employment and higher incomes as well. In this respect, globalisation perhaps is a moral issue after all.

Integration requires economic freedom and trust in technological progress. Again, this is where Liberal thinking is most helpful. Liberals trust not only in market mechanisms, but also in the wisdom of individual decision-making. Opposed to doctrinaire thinking, Liberals do not promise easy answers or simple solutions. Things are not supposed to get easier, they are supposed to get better: these are the words of one of the great old men of German Liberalism, Hans-Dietrich Genscher. Structural change, which accompanies functioning markets, hence globalisation, requires a lot more flexibility from the individual than a system that artificially maintains structures as they are. Thus, Liberal thinking is a constant challenge to our seemingly inborn yearning for constancy and the preservation of the status quo. Of course, it is more popular to protect the immediate short term interests of one's voters. Therefore, governments in the rich countries seem to be more inclined to raise new barriers to the detriment of the poor countries' efforts to reduce poverty.

The trade relations between the European Union and the developing countries is one case in point, for which even environment and labour rights activists advocate a reform of purely tariff-orientated, and other import-related measures, to further their cause. Indeed, via the International Labour Organisation, and the various multilateral environmental agreements following the 1992 Rio Earth Summit, civil society groups campaigning on a range of these issues have made much headway by pushing for international action and co-operation. In the market economy, the state's role is to set the appropriate signals by its economic policy, to satisfy public needs that the markets cannot provide and to foster social programmes for those who cannot participate in the market process. The problem with globalisation is that, on a global level, there is no state to exert these functions. Thus, the fears of anti-globalisation campaigners who foresee negative developments as in the early days of industrialisation, the so-called Manchester Capitalism that impoverished the working masses, are quite understandable.

Another reason, of course, is the fact that the phenomena of global transactions are neither transparent nor understandable for the general public. For example, the flow of money and short term capital independent from the flow of goods and services is a reason for awe, because it seems to be detached from economic reality and yet has vast implications for the economy of whole regions. Vaclav Havel was right in saying: "We live in a world in which everything is possible and nothing is certain." The lack of transparency and the absence of certainty make one uncomfortable and create the wish for easy answers and simple solutions. Therefore, unfortunately, it is also true that in the anti-globalisation campaigns, the well-intentioned but ill-informed are in some respects being led around by the ill-intentioned and well-informed, as Thomas L. Friedman put it in the New York Times.

The challenge lies in profiting from the benefits of globalisation while limiting its risks. Liberal philosophy is ideally suited for this task because it combines trust in the abilities and the responsibility of the individual with a call for the establishment of a stable institutional framework. Since there is no global state to control and accompany global markets, we have to strengthen international organisations and agreements. Responsibility must be made as global as the markets.

It is no coincidence that the GATT, the General Agreement on Tariffs and Trade, has been turned into a fully-fledged organisation, the WTO. Its aims to ensure fairness of trade rules and regulations and to abolish trade barriers are an ongoing challenge. Negotiations in the framework of WTO are not easy, not only because the issues at hand are complicated but especially because opposing national interests are at stake and have to be reconciled. This is a tedious and cumbersome procedure that takes time, whereas the speed of globalisation seems to increase steadily.

In addition, the stabilisation of the international financial system is an important task on which the IMF should concentrate. We need better means to survey financial transactions, to make economic and financial data more transparent and more comparable. We need standards for solid economic and financial policies that move away from casino capitalism in order to avoid repetition of the Asian crises in the 1990s. Reform must resemble the solid institutional and political framework that national governments are supposed to procure for national economies (*Ordnungspolitik*). But *Ordnungspolitik* in a global world must be careful not to impose rules that keep the developing countries out.

Global responsibility also means tangible solidarity of the industrialised with the less and least developed countries in fighting poverty. First of all, they themselves must take decisive action in tackling the causes of poverty within. This concerns mainly good governance, the rule of law, the termination of armed conflicts, the fight against corruption, the establishment of a market economy and the introduction of functioning social security systems. This is an enormous task, but the rewards are huge.

In his fascinating book, "The Mystery of Capital", the Peruvian economist Hernando de Soto points out interesting examples of the importance of a stable legal framework for the economy. Poverty in developing countries is not necessarily due to a lack of capital as such, but to lack of usable capital. The poor in these countries often have assets but in defective forms. For instance, houses on land without clear title that cannot be used as collateral for loans. Extra-legal assets must therefore be absorbed into the formal system in order to become economically active. This task is too big for most developing countries to take upon their own shoulders. They also need comprehensive support from the international community through capacity building and technology-transfer in the transformation of their political and economic systems. This is in the well-defined interest of the industrialised countries - the history books remind us that Europe was not rebuilt in the aftermath of the Second World War without assistance. Without a measured balance of liberalised trade and governance, the European Recovery Programme would never have survived following the wreckage of the original 1945 Loan Agreement and the consequent controvertibility crisis.

Countries must be given the space to develop at an appropriate speed or risk failure. For it is another misconception that, in a globalised world, companies will necessarily shift their production sites to poor countries with weak governments in order to profit from low labour costs, low taxes and the absence of regulations. For an investor, the level of productivity is just as important as the level of labour cost, and a stable framework provided by the state is no less valuable than low tax levels. A well trained labour force in a stable system of social peace and security is a considerable asset.

Governments therefore play an important part in the competitiveness of national economies. Thus, economic policies of national governments in a globalised world are not superfluous. By having to compete in creating favourable conditions for investors, they are forced to redirect their actions along the lines of liberal economic philosophy. This is true for industrialised and developing countries alike.

Overwhelming debt is a serious impediment to development. Therefore debt relief is a crucial element of solidarity with underdeveloped countries. Important steps have been taken with the help of the IMF and the World Bank in the framework of the enhanced Initiative for the Heavily Indebted Poor Countries (HIPC), which also led to the complete waiving of bilateral debt by some G7 countries. The aim is to establish a solid basis for long term debt sustainability, in order to avoid a situation where a country is choked by servicing its foreign debt. This initiative is therefore only a beginning. But the remission of debt is not a panacea. Credit is an essential element of all economic systems. It can only work on the basis of trust and the mutual understanding that, in principle, loans are being paid back.

The most important aspect of solidarity is the opening of markets for the products of developing countries. Growth is crucial in the fight against poverty. There is no better aid than trade. It is a mere absurdity, for example, that the OECD countries spend 360 billion dollars annually for agricultural subsidies while refusing to allow the import of agricultural products from developing countries. It has been said that the whole African continent could sink beneath the waves of the ocean without the rest of the world being affected economically.

This statement shows that being cut off from the global economy is a verdict of doom. Developing countries need more globalisation, not less.

Industrialised countries must open their borders for the products of the Third World. The European Commission's initiative "Everything but Arms", which calls for the complete abolition of import customs for all goods except arms from the 48 least developed countries, is a first step which must be followed by others. The example of countries like China, shows that one of the best ways for poor countries to develop is through exporting cheaply produced goods. The development strategy of "import substitution," on the other hand, has had disastrous results.

Perhaps the best example for the benefits of steps towards globalisation is the European Union. From its beginnings as the European Community for Coal and Steel in 1951, it has progressed steadily, albeit not always on a direct path, in cutting back impediments to the free flow of people, goods, services and capital. The Common Market, though still incomplete, has boosted vastly the participating countries' economies. The development of a country like Portugal, once the poor man of Europe, into a modern and prosperous society is an impressive example.

The European Union, to be sure, has taken a long time and still has a long way to go. Not all of its policies are designed to tackle the phenomenon of globalisation. It sets a bad example with its centralised agricultural policy, which is anything but market based, and for largely denying access to agricultural products from outside. But, as an example of the beneficial effects of freeing market forces in a framework of solidarity, it is simply striking. Those who protest against the democratic deficit apparent in the processes and institutions of globalisation should instead direct their energies into contributing to a globalised world in which every nation, every region and every individual can participate.

The European Social Model, Globalisation and Reform

Anne Jensen

The strongest opposition to international capital movements and free trade is based on the presumption that economic globalisation compels social market systems to dismantle themselves in order to be able to compete with those economies that have the highest degree of human misery, no regard for the protection of natural resources, and thus the lowest level of social and labour costs, as well as costs for environmental protection.

Market forces are said to threaten social protection and stability in the rich world and prevent the development of better standards of living in the poor countries. The World Trade Organisation is seen as an instrument of an uncontrolled trade liberalisation, which neglects or even hinders any consideration of social, environmental and ethical values. Such thoughts are increasingly put forward by NGOs and political parties, calling for a reversal of the trade liberalisation agenda.

The Liberal answer is that only through a strengthening of competitive power can the social protection of all citizens be secured. In this respect, it is gratifying to note the emphasis European Union leaders have put on this line of policy in the so-called Lisbon Strategy, launched in spring 2000, calling for measures that will make the Union the most competitive economy in ten years. The strategy involves the setting of deadlines for completing the internal market and for liberalising public services. It involves the setting of benchmarks and exchange of best practices in research and educational policies, with special attention to the use of information technology. In addition, it involves coordination, benchmarking and exchange of best practice in social policies, with special focus on social exclusion and the challenges for the economy in the form of ageing populations.

This policy certainly has a Liberal stamp on it, but unfortunately some of the Liberal elements lack popular support and can be carried out only if politicians are brave and able to convince the electorate that what might seem difficult in the short term is the right policy in the longer term. Of course, it is easy to understand that French workers who have lost their jobs because of local production moving to other parts of the world must conceive free market forces and globalisation as the problem. These fears reflect the threat that some people see building against the European social model as a result of globalisation. However, free market forces are not the problem but rather the solution to securing a high social standard for Europe in the future.

From my own experience, coming from a small country, Denmark, which represents the Scandinavian "cradle to the grave" society seen by many people as the perfection of the European social model, it seems pretty clear that most threats to this social model come from within, from flaws in the model rather than from forces outside, though on the surface it might sometimes look differently. The internal challenges for our system of social protection - such as the ageing population and changed family structures putting huge financial strain on the system - will best be coped with by changing the system to provide more emphasis on individual responsibility, improving incentives for work, and improving freedom of choice in services from the social and health care systems.

The European Social Model and Free Trade

Some of us might prefer to deny the existence of a European Social Model. However, despite many differences in social protection systems in the EU and in the outside world, there are some similarities. All member states have a rather high level of social protection instituted by law, although the protection systems are organised differently. We talk about the Scandinavian, the Anglo-Saxon and the Continental models, but even this distinction is rather inaccurate. The social models of Europe often face common challenges, such as globalisation, technological change and the problems presented by ageing populations.

The concept of work is altering rapidly due to changes in working patterns, work organisation and skill requirements. In the future, the key to success will be greater adaptability. Achieving this means striking a balance between flexibility for enterprises and security for employees; promoting new forms of work organisation and technology whilst preserving decent, safe and healthy working conditions. It is wrong to see the effects of globalisation and new technology as determinants of misery when these developments bring opportunities for improved living conditions and higher standards of living. Ricardo's classical argument, for the exploitation of comparative advantage in free trade to the benefit of all, still holds good. Let me give one example: the textile industries in the European Union and in Denmark in particular.

The textile industries in the EU have suffered huge job losses over the last 20-30 years even though the European Union has long kept strict quotas on imports of cheap clothing from poor Third World countries with low wages. This is true in Denmark as elsewhere, but Denmark has taken a markedly different approach. The Danish textile industry has thrived by using a strategy of keeping design and development at home, transferring most of the production to low-wage countries, but preserving domestic 'buffer' production, which becomes useful when there is larger than expected demand or problems with supply. High quality is the Danish trademark.

Production still based in Denmark is highly technological, or based on a well-educated, flexible and stable labour force. This works well because of the good social relations that are a tradition of the Danish labour market, reinforced during the last twenty years in which employees generally have come to feel far more loyalty to their employer than to the European Union. The social dialogue in Denmark is thus of a rather decentralised and liberal nature and not the centralised concrete-type Rhineland-model most people associate with the concept of social dialogue.

The region where the textile industry in Denmark is located has benefited strongly in economic terms from this strategy. There are fewer women employed in the traditional and hard job of sewing. They have employment in others sectors of the economy, such as the service industry. And new jobs have been created in the low wage countries, mainly Poland, the Baltic States and Portugal, providing investment opportunities, modern work organisation and increased prosperity to these countries.

What lessons can be drawn from this example? Competing in a global economy requires high performance enterprises with a high performance workforce. It is no solution to deplore or fight changing conditions. As consumers, we want the best products at the most advantageous prices. Therefore we must accept the other side of the coin, and adapt to change. The key to success is to strike the right balance between flexibility and security. Employers need to see greater flexibility, in particular more interchangeable skills among their employees and adaptable working patterns, while employees need assurances about their own employability and job prospects. Better organisation of work can offer workers increased security through greater involvement in the organisation of work, a greater choice of working arrangements, more job satisfaction and the possibility of developing skills and long term employability. In turn, this provides employers with increased flexibility in the form of a more skilled and motivated labour force, better able to take the initiative, to cope with change and to be more deeply involved in the economic health of the company. That is Liberal social policy, and a good social dialogue has a key role in achieving the right balance.

Social Policy and an 'Ageing Europe'

Demographic trends mean that the workforce and the population of the European Union are, on average, getting older. The changing balance between the working and the retired population poses a major challenge to economic and social cohesion - probably a bigger challenge than most of the perceived threats of globalisation.

The main issues at stake are the sustainability of pension systems and the future provision for health care systems. The reform of pension systems has long been on the agenda among those macro-economists and politicians concerned about the sustainability of 'pay as-you-go' pension systems. These discussions must consider options to cope with a growing number of retired people in proportion to the number of people in the workforce providing the funding for these pension schemes. Though the extent of the potential problem differs very much between countries, there are also similarities.

A general recommendation has been to develop pension schemes based on three pillars - a basic compulsory scheme covering all; supplementary employment-related funded schemes; and individual funded schemes. Such a three pillar system should be more robust than the present schemes as it could combine the 'pay-as-you-go' system, where individual responsibility is accentuated, with some measure of mutual insurance. After all it should not come as a surprise to any of us that if you have the luck to live a long life, you will eventually grow old and grey and be in need of pension and care. So from a moral standpoint it is fairly easy to argue in favour of more personal responsibility for the provision for old-age support.

The 'pay-as-you-go' systems were built by poor societies, where little was saved by most of the population. Many of these have gone on to become richer nations, whose elderly feel entitled to a fairer share. Today it would be difficult for the vast majority of the employed population in the EU to argue that they cannot find the means for pension saving schemes.

Funded schemes are widespread in only a few countries in the EU such as the United Kingdom, Netherlands and Denmark. And 'tomorrow's problem' in some countries like Italy, with a faltering and unsustainably expensive pension system, is already 'today's problem'. However, apart from the United Kingdom, which has a rather small public financial provision for retired people, all EU members will need to increase substantially contributions from young people in the workforce unless the system is changed.

Some people still argue against these kinds of reform, claiming that the demographic forecasts are very uncertain, and that technical change and productivity gains may completely change the picture. They also argue against the reforms for political reasons, fearing that the solidarity of the present systems will disappear or be diminished. But they tend to forget the solidarity between generations, which should work both ways. For many years in the 1970's and 1980's, present generations prepared a legacy for future generations consisting of huge state debts, low investments in infrastructure and low birth-rates. A bitter cocktail indeed for our children to drink. It is a good thing that political winds have changed in a more responsible direction.

The funded pension schemes will provide the basis for a larger and more liquid capital market in Europe, thus providing the basis for stronger capital formation and growth i.e. securing the wealth that will pay for future pensions. The EU today has a population and economy much the same size as that of the USA, but a market share only one third of the size. Capital formation in the EU is to a large extent done through banks. But raising more capital through the open market will be beneficial for the competitiveness and dynamics of business life in the EU in the future.

It is not just pension schemes but also health provision and care systems which will be affected by ageing populations. Coupled with increased female participation in the workforce and changing patterns of family life, these changes will have profound implications for Europe's employment and social protection systems. The focus until now has mainly been on the economic consequences of the rising cost of health care and long term care needs of dependent older people. How to fund the system? One answer given is that more people should be in the work force in order to support the cost. It may be one response, but is a very simplistic answer to a very complicated problem.

In Denmark you find the highest employment rate in the European Union, because Danish women have an employment rate only slightly below that of men. Even young mothers have a very high employment rate, made possible by the public provision of day-care for children. On the other hand the Danish labour market is very divided by sex, with women and men working in different areas of the economy, and women mostly taking care of the tasks they used to take care of in the informal economy, such as child care and the care of sick and elderly persons.

It is striking that the things we should rationally and emotionally rank of the highest value in life - questions of how we get into this world; how we secure a childhood with love, security and affection; and of how we get out of this world whilst being cared for with compassion - seem to have no value. All we talk about is economic costs, never value. In the future, however, I believe that care of quality and value will be in greater demand, and we already see this tendency in Denmark. Having for many years had a system of huge public care provision, focus has switched from quantity to quality, and people now increasingly demand individual solutions and influence on the organisation of care. Healthcare, as well as child care and care for the elderly, is under fiscal pressure, and there is a growing understanding that new solutions must be found for the future.

These solutions should be Liberal solutions, introducing competition to improve quality, reintroducing individual responsibility and, most of all, giving freedom of choice between different solutions. The high level of social protection is very popular, even though it is expensive for the taxpayer and will be burdensome for the economy in the future. Therefore, a much stronger focus should be put on value for taxpayers' money.

The Liberal Way

The political winds have changed so much that the Danish population today believes that Liberal parties are better able to secure the future welfare state than the Social Democrats. That is an entirely new popular understanding in a country where the Socialist parties have previously been viewed as the guardians of the welfare state. Today, the Socialists have connected their policies to preserving the status quo - denying any problems and not listening to the wishes of parents, or of patients or the elderly - and the call has grown for the need to introduce new steering mechanisms in the social and health sector. Voucher systems - letting the money follow the patient or the child - would introduce better incentives into the systems of public services. Allowing private providers of public services to compete with the public provider of that service, thus challenging the present system, is the Liberal way.

Being a Liberal, I find it difficult to see any conflict between a liberal economic environment and a society with high social standards, as well as high standards of environment protection. On the contrary, it seems obvious today that you find the highest standard of living in societies built on Liberal values, on democracy and individual freedom and rights, including economic freedom. In that sense, Liberalism has conquered.

Of course, markets are not perfect outside of the models found in the textbooks. Even Liberals accept that some intervention and regulation is necessary. Market forces should be seen as an instrument, not a God, and this instrument should work within a suitable regulatory framework. But as an instrument, market forces reflect the joint outcome of many peoples' different decisions. It is therefore a very democratic instrument of rule, and intervention should be for the purposes of securing the beneficial side of free markets rather than combating the very role of market forces. Increasingly, both the will of populations and the economic textbooks tell us that the consumer is the king. Well if this king has wisdom, sufficient knowledge and strong ethical values, he should govern wisely.

Addressing Globalisation's Critics: The World's Poor Need Less ATTAC and More Globalisation

Cecilia Malmström

Why is the concept of free trade so provoking? What are the issues that make international summits, such as the WTO Ministerial in Seattle, the EU summits in Nice and Gothenburg and the G8 in Genoa inspire young people from all over the world to demonstrate and protest against a variety of targets, particularly that phenomenon known as globalisation? Some of the protesters are 'professional demonstrators' whose politics are a pretext for hooligan behaviour. However, it would be dishonest to describe the majority in this manner. 30,000 peaceful demonstrators came to the EU summit in my home town of Gothenburg, most connected to the anti-globalisation movement, environmental organisations, churches or labour and human rights groups: an astonishingly broad coalition from ATTAC[6] to the World Council of Churches. Such groups have used the media attention related to the meetings to promote vigorously their dislike of free trade, the EU, the capitalist system or to express worries about closed borders, environmental issues or Third World debt. The main enemy seems to be the liberal system and the financial markets, the latter characterised as some abstract evil that desperately needs to be tamed.

Concern about people who are less privileged, whether in our own countries or abroad, is an important pillar of Liberal ideology. In my late teens, I decided to join the Liberal party in Sweden because I was attracted by its message of individual freedom combined with social responsibility. Having, at that age, very clear views on the world, I was involved actively in questions regarding international solidarity. The

---

[6] Association for the Taxation of Financial Transactions for the Aid of Citizens.

Swedish Liberal party was very firm in supporting democratic values around the world and in the need to help the poorer world to develop into democratic and economically sustainable societies via aid and trade. I was attracted to the Folkpartiet because of its long tradition in fighting for Liberal priorities such as generous development aid, human rights, free trade, generous asylum policies and EU membership.

The Liberal party had concrete ideas on how to achieve a better world by focusing on the important combination of economic development, democracy and human rights. This was in sharp contrast to the parties on the left who saw the whole world as a class conflict. The Swedish Communist Party has always been against Swedish membership in all possible international organisations (EFTA, EES, Partnership for Peace, EU etc). The left's way of making the economy develop is not via international cooperation and free trade, but rather by strict barriers, protectionism and quotas.

The demonstrations at international meetings, but also the public debate in general, show that there is a growing tendency among young people to protest against current trends with regard to international solidarity, environment and global inequalities. Everybody involved in politics should welcome this engagement as it is based on a frustration we share, namely that, despite overall progress, there is still much poverty, misery and violation of human rights all over the planet. The global distribution of income is becoming ever more unequal. The demonstrations and the debate in the press point a finger at globalisation as being to blame for all these injustices.

Numerous groups have sprung up as a part of the anti-globalisation movement. ATTAC has emerged as one of the most vocal critics of economic globalisation and it is attracting the young and politically-engaged from all over the world. The proposal to change the world, advocated by ATTAC, is to institute a tax on financial transactions in the global capital markets, a so-called Tobin tax named after its inventor, the Nobel Prize winner and economist James Tobin. The idea of the Tobin tax is to stem speculative and often irrational and destabilising capital flows and raise money to correct some of the wrongs attributed to globalisation. More regulations, closed borders, control of the global markets and less free trade: some of these arguments sound like old-fashioned Marxism in a new suit. Let us have a closer look at the arguments.

Tobin Himself Does Not Believe in the Tobin Tax

James Tobin introduced the concept of a common, worldwide tax on financial transactions back in 1972. The Chief Editor of France's Le Monde Diplomatique, Ignacio Ramonet, reawakened the idea when he took the initiative that led to the creation of the ATTAC movement. The movement proposes a levy of 0.5% on all financial transactions and that this money be used for the "common good" such as paying the debts of the Third World. Unfortunately, the Tobin tax is not feasible.

First and foremost, in order to make a Tobin tax functional, every country of the world would have to agree to the idea and establish a firm control mechanism on a global level in order to prevent a few countries from operating as 'tax paradises.' We have already learnt from the failure of recent efforts addressed at offshore banking havens that economic and political realities prevent us achieving such idealistic concepts. Moreover, the Tobin tax may not be economically desirable. It would not stop fluctuations of the markets, which result from a wide variety of different influences. The Tobin tax would make it even more expensive for small companies to insure themselves against the effects of such fluctuations. Risky investment, often in poor countries, would be much more expensive to the disadvantage of the poorer world.

Professor Tobin himself does not see globalisation as something evil. In his article "Financial Globalisation" written in 1998, he writes, "globalisation of the financial markets, the liberalisation and deregulation of international financial transactions have, in a way, contributed to economic progress in the developing world".

However, Mr Ramonet and his co-editor Bernard Cassen see no advantages in globalisation. They want to restrict consumption and insist on the so-called 'localisation agenda': that all goods should be produced and consumed locally. These are very old-fashioned proposals that beg the question of what such an agenda would have done for the so-called 'Asian tigers' and for Japan with very little of its own production of agriculture and food. Countries like North Korea and Cuba illustrate the fallacy of isolationism. Less trade does not lead to prosperity and democracy.

Curiously, many of those protesting against globalisation champion an economic model that would promote the European Common Agricultural Policy. The French farmer José Bové, member of ATTAC and an opponent to globalisation, is well known for his protests against McDonalds. His proposal is for totally regulated agriculture with fixed prices, production quotas and high tariffs. He is passionately against free trade and thinks that the Third World should be self-supplying with regard to agriculture.

The way to strengthen democracy and economic development can still be found in the old Liberal proposals: open markets, free trade and cooperation achieve development. Globalisation as a rule is positive for the whole world. It leads to economic development, growth, innovation, democracy and interdependence. More and more people are convinced by the advantages of openness and the free exchange of goods, capital and information. Positive exchange of technology, new ideas and culture is also due to globalisation.

While far too many states still restrict democracy, information about violations of human rights is spread all over the world. For instance, Chinese students and human rights defenders can pass their message across the world via the internet, a tool that the authorities desperately, and in vain, try to control. As China becomes more involved in the multilateral trading system and other international fora, it will become harder for the authorities to stop progress towards democratic change.

human beings and the environment. It is Liberal policies that lead to emancipation and economic development, not the isolation and closed borders that constitute the alternative.

The Case for Universalism[7]

Annemie Neyts-Uyttebroeck

As the challenges of globalisation, the shouting of its critics and its loudest apostles, become characterised by the retreat of many into old ideological bunkers, it is worth while to reflect on what Liberalism has to offer us. I would like to share some thoughts with you on the following question. Do we, Liberals, offer a unique, irreplaceable and therefore indispensable approach to present day world affairs, or do we have nothing better to offer than diluted environmentalism, toned down social democracy, watered down conservatism, or some revisited third way approach?

Today, having lived through more than half a century, I am able to answer the question in what I hope will be a satisfactory manner. Need I say that this was not the case when I first became a liberal activist? In those years, my liberal beliefs were more like a mindset, more of an inclination bred by my upbringing, fostered by my marriage to a Liberal and strengthened by the friendship and sympathy of many other Liberals. A mindset, a state of mind. The one so beautifully described by Gladstone, and engraved on the pedestal of his bust in the entrance hall of the National Liberal Club, "Conservatism is mistrust of people, qualified by fear. Liberalism is trust in people, qualified by prudence."

Trust in people lies at the root of liberalism. Now you may ask, do only liberals put trust in people? Of course not. Nor are only liberals trustworthy, nor, I must add, are all self-avowed liberals trustworthy. However, no other ideology is so fundamentally rooted in trust in people as liberalism is. Every ideology stemming from a

---

[7] Adapted from the 2001 Isaiah Berlin Lecture, 25 June 2001 given by Annemie Neyts-Uyttebroeck.

transcendental worldview, rests on the submission of man and woman to some grand design not of their own making. Whether the grand design originates from a religion, or may be aimed at the realisation of some man-made plan, it will be imposed upon the people, and the people will be expected or forced to submit to it. Ideologies of this type deny people the fundamental freedom to govern their own lives, or allow it only within tight boundaries.

So no grand design, no transcendence, no finality of history - Francis Fukuyama notwithstanding - for Liberals? No indeed. Liberals entrust people with the task of shaping their own lives, communities and societies and expect to be entrusted with the same responsibilities. It is precisely this unique approach that is best suited to the political and economic challenges we face in the era of economic globalisation.

Need I stress the strong appeal of grand designs? Socialism, even in its much weakened form of the Left (la Gauche in French, New Labour in English) survives all the evidence of failure inflicted upon it by recent history. Michail Gorbachev once told me that Russia would have been much better off if the 1917 Revolution had stopped in February, and not gone on to the October Revolution. He is certainly right, but the images reconstructed by Eisenstein prevail up to this very day. Yet, all over the world we see avowedly socialist governments such as New Labour in Britain bow to the liberal consensus in both their economic and political agenda. Britain also provides us with an example of the crushing irrelevance of conservative parties that formerly hijacked neo-liberal economics, but had since failed to move with the liberal social and cultural changes, leaving the party nothing more than an empty ideological space.

As the liberal mindset is one based on trust (qualified by prudence) in people, the basic attitude is one of confidence in man and woman, in every man and every woman, in every part of the world. Such a political approach also entrusts each woman and man with the right, the task, the responsibility to shape her and his own life and does not subject them to any ready made design or plan. This is no easy undertaking. The hurdles are many, and some of them are our own biases and prejudices. Let me take our attitude to developing countries as an example, and let me start with an anecdote.

Last year, when I last met Sam Rainsy, the Opposition leader in Cambodia, he had a telling story that underlines my point. As Sam Rainsy was travelling the world to meet Cambodian exiles, he encountered a Cambodian farmer in New Zealand, who said, "Cambodia once was a rich country. It had everything: fertile soils, dense forests, game, gems, talented people, a great history and culture. Communism took all that away and today Cambodia and the Cambodians live in poverty and misery. New Zealand has only grasslands and pastures, but New Zealand and the New Zealanders are rich. That is because they are free." (I could add, "and because an enlightened Labour Prime Minister, Mike Moore, turned New Zealand into the most liberalised country in the world," but I must not stray). Sam Rainsy's farmer had coined a great truth: individual freedom is the key to development, and it is a universal key. Does that sound naïve; does that sound so simple that you have discarded it even before I finished the sentence?

Well, think again. Liberal presidents such as Abdoulaye Wade from Senegal and Chen Shui Bian from Taiwan, Liberal leaders like Sam Rainsy and so many others have put their lives at risk, have served prison terms, because they hold the view that freedom is not a privilege reserved for those in power. They not only hold this view, they have acted accordingly, and that of course is why they met with fierce opposition and persecution from those in power.

I, like so many others, thought for quite some time that fundamental civil liberties (such as freedom of speech, assembly and worship, economic freedom and political freedom) were non-essential rights, luxury rights so to say, the fulfilment of which could only follow the fulfilment of really vital needs like food, shelter and education. Why did I ever think that freedom and liberty were fundamental to me and to my fellow citizens, but not for those born in other parts of the world? Why didn't I see sooner that freedom does not develop from development, but that development develops from freedom?

It is hardly an excuse that the view 'first development, and only then (eventually) freedom' was, and still is, common wisdom. This view, which generally suits those in power in developing countries, explains to a large extent the colossal failure of Western development aid. The prejudice and the bias we need to free ourselves from, is that freedom, individual initiative and civil liberties are results of development. We need to do away with the illusion that development should come first. We need to stress and spread the view that freedom, individual initiative and civil liberties are the very tools of development.

In order to provide for the framework in which freedom, individual initiative and civil liberties can thrive, democracy and the rule of law are essential, and therefore we must continue to insist on the need to put them in place. We now witness a growing recognition of the universality of these most basic rights, but that does not mean these rights are universally accepted or respected yet. The simple fact of the growing membership of Liberal International, with more than eighty parties in more than seventy countries in the world, testifies to this growing recognition, but the battle is far from won.

Consider, for instance, the situation of women. Entire cultures and religions deny women the most basic rights. The plight of women in Afghanistan and Pakistan is appalling, and worsening as Jasma Jahangir, the latest laureate of Liberal International's Prize for Freedom, told me last autumn.

What nation has the courage to put at risk its mineral and geopolitical interest by speaking out against the fate of women in Saudi Arabia or Iran? Well, the European Union did make the government representatives of the Gulf Co-operation Council pledge to respect the equality of men and women, and that is how progress starts: first by mere declarations. This growing recognition of the value of individual freedom fuels the growth of political liberalism. Every setback of that recognition is a threat to the development of political liberalism. More importantly, it is a threat to the peaceful development of humankind. I can think of many such possible setbacks: some are developing under our very eyes, in this part of the world.

The Third Way, for example, which is conservatism disguised as new socialism, to smother liberalism. Or shall I evoke the irrational rejection of free trade?

You have certainly watched the broadcasts from Göteborg and Genoa, the violence in the streets, but more importantly, the thousands of peaceful young demonstrators. I respect peaceful demonstrators, but I cannot help but be amazed by the return of the demons of my own student days as the objects of these protests. Liberalism runs the risk of being overwhelmed by this growing protest movement, unless we develop an intelligent answer to it. We should avoid two errors. Error number one: howl with the crowds, be it in a slightly more civilised way.

The masochism of the European Union is a case in point. Why should people support an institution, which its leaders themselves ceaselessly call inefficient, insufficiently transparent, insufficiently accountable, suffering from democratic deficit, and so on? No wonder the Irish stayed at home or came out mainly to say, no, thank you.

Error number two: tackle the players rather than the ball. Fight the arguers, the demonstrators, rather than the arguments. Most of the demonstrators are being manipulated by old leftist groups, which had gone into hibernation and now re-emerge, smelling new battles.

Denouncing them will not make the arguments disappear. One overwhelming concern of the young demonstrators is the gap between the developed world and the developing world. They are being told that the market economy, commerce, trade and capitalism are to blame. Liberalism has, of old, been associated with each of those, and rightly so, because they all are tools of development. That means that the protest against Liberalism cannot be far away. We must not try to dissociate ourselves from what we rightly view as tools of development, we must stress relentlessly that this is what they are, "tools of development", and that it is the development which matters. We must add that they do not suffice to insure sustainable political development but that democracy and the rule of law are needed in developing countries too.

As an international movement, Liberal International must continue to reach out to political parties and their leaders in developing countries. We must continue to assemble and work there, with the local parties and leaders. This newly emerging protest movement is not the only threat to political liberalism. Another threat is posed by those, in our own countries and elsewhere, who reject the very notion of universality, who believe in cultural, linguistic and ethnic purity, and who spread the view that cultures, languages and nations should keep to themselves and should on no account mix, lest they lose their identity and authenticity.

Need I stress that both strands of protest beautifully merge into one single protest against globalisation?

Again the above-mentioned errors must be avoided, but the case for universality, openness, cross-cultural and cross-national co-operation should be easier, at least in theory. The latest developments in Northern Ireland and in Macedonia show how difficult it is to overcome centuries of prejudice, discrimination and separate development. That is true in Europe. And it is no more, or no less true outside Europe, in Indonesia for instance, or in Central Africa. The very reason for these tragic developments is not the openness or the universality, but the lack of openness and the absence of universality. Globalisation is not the culprit, but the absence of perspective beyond one's own village, one's own community, settlement, religion, ethnic origin, and language…

The case for universalism is our case.

I have tried to show that Liberalism offers a unique, indispensable and irreplaceable approach to world affairs because it is rooted in trust, because it entrusts people with the right and the plight to shape their own lives and communities, because it considers that individual freedom and individual initiative are the indispensable tools of development. I have also shown that this approach is universally valid, if not universally accepted. I have pointed to several threats posed to Liberalism by recent developments, in Europe and elsewhere, and have indicated how, in my view, these threats should be countered. The battle for Liberalism is far from won, but it is a most worthwhile battle, because it is the battle for the recognition of the universal right to individual freedom.

Freedom and Responsibility from a Dutch Social Liberal Perspective: Social Liberal Questions in the Face of a Globalised World[8]

Lousewies van der Laan

It was not without fascination that many political observers watched the riots in Seattle surrounding the World Trade Organisation (WTO) annual meeting on 30 November 1999. Though the violence of a few must be strongly condemned, there was something revolutionary, even inspiring about individuals and grassroots organisations taking on the power of governments and industry. Earlier that year, Burger King was forced to close one of its restaurants in an Israeli settlement in the Palestinian Territories, because one angry email had spiralled into a global barrage of letters to its management. In February 2000, when Warner Brothers threatened closure of private 'Harry Potter'[9] websites because of copyright infringements, Harry Potter fans were so outraged they organised a worldwide boycott of Warner Brothers' products.

When individuals take on established power, and especially when they manage to effect change, it is music to the ears of Liberals. Liberals have a fundamental distrust of power. The only way to halt power's tendency to corrupt is by ensuring that it is given temporarily, is controllable and can be taken away again by those over whom it is exerted. It is precisely these safeguards that are missing in today's globalised world.

More and more decisions are taken at a level of power far removed

---

[8] This article has benefited from the recent publication of 'Sociaal-liberalisme, pragmatisme en radicale democratisering: het D66 debat', by Dennis Hesseling and Herman Beun, in *Een Vierde Weg? Links liberalisme als traditie en als orietatiepunt,* 2001 (VUB Press) and I thank the authors for their support.
[9] Harry Potter is a fictional character in hugely popular books about a young magician's apprentice.

from citizens, not just constitutionally speaking but also geographically. The European Union's Council of Ministers is one regional example of a body that is largely free of democratic control, especially in areas like agriculture, foreign policy and fighting crime, whose powers profoundly affect the daily lives of European citizens. Europe's agricultural policy, which represents more than one third of its annual budget, is decided by qualified majority voting without any parliament, either national or European, having any say over the outcome. We find the same at global level in the WTO, the G7 and numerous agencies and quangos (quasi-autonomous non-governmental organisations). These are institutions that take decisions influencing people's lives, beyond democratic accountability. Often seeming deliberately obscure to their critics, institutions such as the WTO have proved unwilling to engage in a broad democratic debate over their function and objectives.

Decisions passed in these bodies, including global agreements like MAI[10] and TRIPS[11], should not be passed without people's knowledge and influence. It is therefore not without reason that the protestors tried to make their voice heard at the 1999 WTO Ministerial meeting in Seattle. However, the alternatives they propose are often both unrealistic and undesirable. The real challenge for Liberals is how to embrace and encourage regional and global efforts of nations to work together, while not losing sight of minimum requirements of democracy. It is for drawing attention to this dilemma that Liberals should be thankful to the Seattle demonstrators. The protests drew wide scale public attention to a decision-making process that until then had been almost unnoticed.

At the dawn of the 21st Century, Liberals have to ask themselves what contribution they can make to face the challenges ahead. Globalisation brings with it an incredible development potential as markets open up, and people and nations start working together on a regional and global scale. The liberalisation of world trade has not only brought economic advances, it also brings people closer together.

---

[10] Multilateral Agreement on Investment.
[11] Trade-Related Aspects of Intellectual Property Rights.

It will become increasingly difficult for Indonesia to deny its people basic human rights when these can call for help via the Internet or have the violations broadcast live on CNN. At the same time, international crime, illegal traffic in human beings and drugs, environmental pollution and extinction of animal and plant species are on the rise as a result of our shrinking world. The people affected by these and other tragedies hardly ever have the means to fight against these developments.

From the Russian farmer who can not sell his cattle because the EU had dumped the European beef surplus on the Russian market in the guise of "humanitarian aid", to the politicians who cannot get animal testing for cosmetics banned in Europe because the WTO does not allow for such a "limitation on trade", people everywhere feel they are losing grip on their lives. How can Liberals continue to support trade liberalisation through the WTO and European integration led by the Council of Ministers, without losing their liberal values?

How to deal with these developments depends on one's view of power, one's vision of people and especially one's acceptance of the regulatory role of the state in limiting some of the excesses of economic freedom. It is here that Liberalism divides into two schools - utilitarian or conservative Liberalism on the one hand and development, or Social, or left Liberalism on the other. The former deals primarily with economic freedom and finds its proponents in Locke, Hume, Smith and the American federalists. These Liberals have a negative definition of freedom - people should be free of restrictions and impediments, usually imposed by governments. The other Liberal school knows that true liberty will not be achieved merely by an absence of restrictions. People equally need to be stimulated to emancipate and develop themselves. They find their representatives in Kant, von Humboldt, John Stuart Mill and more recently Isaiah Berlin, Karl Popper and Ralf Dahrendorf[12].

To fully understand this distinction and its implications for dealing

---

[12] For a more detailed analysis, see *Een Vierde Weg? over drie vormen van links-liberalisme,* Patrick Stouthuysen, *ibidem.*

with globalisation it is helpful to know how Liberalism developed in the Netherlands and why the Dutch, like the Danes and Norwegians have two Liberal parties – right wing, or conservative Liberals and left wing, or social Liberals.

A Short History of Social Liberalism in the Netherlands[13]

Apart from Georgia, the Netherlands is the only European country where city Mayors are not democratically elected but appointed by the national government. The Dutch cannot elect their Prime Minister, who is appointed by the Queen. And the Netherlands is one of only five democracies in the world never to have held a national referendum, because the constitution does not allow for this possibility.

This may come as a surprise to many. For centuries after all, the Netherlands has also been one of the most Liberal countries in Europe. Freedom of religion and conscience were the founding ideas of the Dutch Republic when it set off, much like today's EU, as a loose confederation of independent states in 1579. With less than two million inhabitants at the time, the United Republic did not only become an economic, technological and military superpower that played an important role in the globalisation of world trade, it also provided a safe haven for those being persecuted in other countries. It is not a coincidence that so many great, but at the time controversial thinkers, like Erasmus, Spinoza, Descartes and Voltaire, lived, worked or published their works in the Netherlands.

In 20th Century Dutch history, there is a long tradition of progressive politics. In 1966, in the middle of the roaring sixties, Dutch society was eager for democratisation and more participation of citizens. Not only dissident Liberals and Social Democrats, but also non-partisans, joined in forming a new party, *Democraten '66* (D66)[14]. The new party urged radical reforms. Voters should get more influence on policy by means of constitutional reform. The party wanted (and wants) to

---

[13] Taken partly from the D66 website with thanks to Wilfried Derksen and Ralph de Vries.

[14] The apostrophe was later removed and the party is now called D66.

achieve this by introducing measures such as an elected Prime Minister, elected mayors and stronger bonds between voters and members of Parliament, for example, through multi-member constituencies. The party consciously sought to break the hold of traditional class and religious alignments in favour of a far-reaching programme of institutional reform. D66 participated for the first time in the elections of 1967. The result was spectacular: four and a half percent of the popular vote, meaning seven seats out of 150 in Parliament. A new political force was born.

Social Liberalism - the Political Freedom Axes

Since the party's birth, D66 has been trying to explain where it stands in the political spectrum. Being undogmatic, refusing until 2000 to put down its founding principles, did not help clarify matters to the voter. It was Erwin Nypels, one of the founders of the party, who made a first serious attempt by creating the attached diagram (Fig. 1) to illustrate where Social Liberals position themselves with respect to other political currents. It was not until 1998 that D66 finally formally adopted the subtitle 'Social Liberal'.[15]

Immaterial axis	Social Liberals
Socialists	Conservative
	Liberals
Communists	*Material axis*
	Christian Democrats
Figure 1	Conservatives

---

[15] For a detailed analysis of this process see: 'Social-liberalisme, pragmatisme en radicale democratisering: het D66 debat', by Dennis Hesseling and Herman Beun, in *Een Vierde Weg? Links liberalisme als traditie en als orientatiepunt,* 2001 (VUB Press).

The horizontal axis of this cross represents material (social-economic) freedom. This axis is the best known political classification, and symbolises the classical left versus right divide in politics. On the right side of this axis, i.e. with a high score in the area of material freedom, are parties that place high value on the free market (Conservative - Liberals, Thatcherites). Parties that believe that the government should exercise firm control over the economy score low in the area of material freedom and find themselves on the left hand of the axis (Social Democrats, Socialists, Communists).

The vertical axis symbolises immaterial freedom. The placing of parties along this axis indicates to what extent parties feel that citizens should be able to take moral responsibility over their lives. A high score on this axis indicates that a party believes the people should be able to decide for themselves over issues such as abortion, euthanasia and drug use (Social Liberals). Parties that are critical towards legalisation of these issues score low on the immaterial axis, therefore placing themselves at the bottom end (Conservatives, Christian Democrats).

Democratisation is part of the immaterial axis. Not only should the individual be able to decide for him or herself how to organise his or her life, groups and society as a whole can also take decisions that influence their lives. Parties that put a strong emphasis on direct influence of citizens on decision-making, for example by arguing for referenda, but also by encouraging freedom of choice in health and education matters, score high on the immaterial axis. Parties that limit voters' influence to 'have a say' every four years and resist direct public influence on (semi-) public bodies score low on this axis. This latter group seems to include most parties that have been in power for too long. Social Liberals on the other hand recognise that many of their long-term goals can only be achieved if constitutional and institutional reforms take place. It is not without reason that the Liberal Democratic Group in the European Parliament (ELDR)[16] is and has been at the forefront in arguing for reform of the European institutions.

---

[16] www.eldr.org

It is most unfortunate that the two words 'Social Liberal' each have their own meaning and political history. This has allowed less informed parties to caricature Social Liberalism as a bridge between those who want a liberal economy and those who are in favour of strong social policies. In that way, it is diminished into what New Labour and their friends like to call "the Third Way", which of course is nothing more than Socialists finally discovering that Socialism does not work. The Third Way, however, is not the same as Social Liberalism because a combination of market Liberalism and Socialism does not give the citizens more autonomy. In reality, it leads to domination from two sides - the ever more powerful free market on the one hand and a non-transparent government bureaucracy on the other. The challenge for Social Liberals is not to build a bridge between the market and the state, but to change fundamentally the balance of power. It is the citizen who should dominate the market and the state, not the other way around.

Social Liberalism is a concept which stands by itself, with the ability for individuals to choose by themselves as its central tenet.

"D66 focuses on people: free, involved, equal and responsible. We strive for a democratic, sustainable and open society, in which individual freedom is as self-evident as social cohesion; a society in which citizens want to and can take responsibility for themselves and their environment; a society in which work, personal development, free time and care can be combined well. D66 wants to actively create opportunities for people to use their talents and apply their know-how. D66 has faith in the decisions people take about what is dear to them. D66 practises practical and result-oriented politics based on its ideals, without blueprints or dogmas. Decision-making must be verifiable and transparent. .... D66 wants to keep making it possible for people to make their own choices. That is our democratic perspective, that's what we call Social-Liberal."

Excerpt from "The philosophy of D66[17]

---

[17] See D66 website (www.d66.nl) for complete text in English.

Reconciling Globalisation and Democracy

Today's challenge is to apply this Social Liberal philosophy to a globalised world, in which individuals have less and less say over the decision-making processes that affect their lives. The challenge is two-fold because global processes not only evade influence by individuals but are also free of the traditional democratic controls imposed by parliaments. The minimal democratic control exerted by parliaments over global and regional decision-making bodies is hampered by a number of factors.

In the first place, decision-making processes are non-transparent. The classical example of this is the European Council of Ministers, which does not produce minutes or voting accounts of its meetings. No formal trace exists, for example, of High Representative Solana's recent official trip to the Philippines, other than articles in the press relating oral information given at a press conference following the Council meeting. In the second place, national parliaments tend to be so preoccupied with national activities that minimal time is spent on the complicated and non-transparent decision-making processes of far-away bodies. This internal setting of priorities is exacerbated by the not wholly unjustified feeling that it is difficult for individual countries, especially if they are small, to influence the decisions. Thirdly, since the constituents and national press, that tend to dictate politicians' agendas, will not reward activism or achievements in this area, it makes more sense for a politician to focus on other matters. The European Parliament for its part can only influence decision-making where national governments do not have a veto. Whereas this covers a large part of European decision-making, decisions in other international bodies tend to fall outside its remit. It is these factors that have allowed decision-making to slip away to foreign bodies.

This development has not, of course, been discouraged by governments in power, because those with access to the decision-making processes have no interest in sharing power. Once back in the opposition seats, it would be unwise for egotistical reasons for those responsible to admit how much sovereignty has been given away without proper safeguards.

It is clear that democratic control and public accountability is directly related to the degree to which an institution has direct influence on people's lives. It is arguably less urgent, for example, to implement direct public participatory programs over the decisions of the United Nations General Assembly than to increase the transparency and accountability of the EU Council of Ministers. The EU Council of Ministers is the clearest example of a body with direct impact on citizens because it adopts EU legislation, while its decision-making process lacks democratic legitimacy. European agricultural policy, under heavy criticism for its high costs to tax payers, consumers, the environment, animal welfare and the Third World, is decided in the Agricultural Council by qualified majority voting. This means that a majority of EU Member States can overrule the rest. However, whereas qualified majority voting is normally accompanied by a co-decision procedure in which the European Parliament can co-legislate, this is not the case in agriculture. Agriculture accounts for around 40% of the EU budget, but neither national parliaments nor the European Parliament can influence these Council decisions. This means that it is possible for five or six countries, whose tax-payers contribute to the EU budget, to be outvoted, without any democratic checks or balances to the decision. It is bizarre that governments hand over sovereignty in this way to an institution without ensuring the possibility of recourse or re-evaluation. They are paying a high price for it now, both politically and financially. For example, when the Commission decided to slaughter healthy animals arguably in order to increase beef prices across Europe.

How can we try to stop these developments, without turning away from the achievements of European integration or global trade liberalisation? This essay aims to raise questions more than provide answers. Nevertheless, experience shows that there are a number of steps that can be taken to foster at least a minimal level of democratic control.

In order for citizens and national parliaments to be able to exert some kind of control over supranational bodies, they need, in the first place, access to basic information related to decision-making: what is on the agenda, and when, and which texts are on the table for adoption. One institution that has only recently taken this step is the European Parliament. Until last year, draft legislative texts were not available to the general public until they were discussed in committee, by which point it had become too late for civil society to comment. A few Liberal MEPs initiated reform by publishing these texts on their website so that the Parliament was forced to change its policy[18]. The quality of information coming out of the Council of Ministers still depends for a large part on which country holds the Presidency.

Secondly, parliaments, NGOs and the press need to step up pressure on supranational bodies and their members to explain and justify their actions. In order to do that, they need to be knowledgeable, well developed and strong. There are only a few countries whose ministers actually have their hands tied by national parliaments before they jet off to Brussels or Geneva to do business. The quality of these parliaments depends of course on the voters. At the end of the day, it is the voters who must demand high quality parliamentarians who think beyond today's sound bite to the long-term challenges of globalisation.

Thirdly, decision-making in international organisations needs to be simplified, and the checks and balances must be increased, or initiated where they do not exist. The Treaty on European Union's decision-making procedures desperately needs simplification. Last but not least, public accountability and participation in international decision-making needs to be improved. It is hoped that the WTO's intention to involve NGOs in some way in its decision-making is not merely a publicity stunt in order to avoid demonstration. Many NGOs will have valuable and valid points to make and the WTO would be wise to give them an opportunity to share their experiences. At present, the WTO's occasional Symposia and the public relations statements which follow

---

[18] Liberal MEP's Lousewies van der Laan, Nick Clegg, Dirk Sterkcx, Antonio di Pietro and Cecilia Malmström published draft legislative texts on www.OpenUpEurope.com for 7 months before Parliament relented.

do not constitute a genuine 'confronting of the critique'. Nor do such cosmetic admissions of a critical voice recognise the work that must be done in order to open its agenda and decision-making process to the necessary reform and repair.

When Fukuyama announced 'the end of history' with the victory of capitalism over communism, some people falsely assumed that the questions about how to shape our political societies, in this reading, had been answered. In fact, his text does not claim an end to the political processes, and Liberals would be wise to avoid triumphalism and injudicious advocacy of an unqualified 'laissez-faire' neo-liberal economic agenda. The desperate search of left wing governments and parties for a new identity under the guise of 'the Third Way', causing major internal party political divisions, illustrates the increasingly visible tensions evident in political readings of globalisation processes. Indeed, the debate about which political model is best is as fresh as 120 years ago when John Stuart Mill published 'On Liberty'. It is only the actors who have become stale, because they have become accustomed to power and entrenched in their thinking. It means the challenge for Liberals in the 21st Century is greater than ever.

For Social Liberals, the obvious and fairest way to deal with these problems is empowering individuals to keep and to take control over their own lives. This liberal reform must be enacted in such a way that others, be it their government, a large corporation or a drugs syndicate, no longer have the chance to take decisions on their behalf. In a world where governments and markets are the main players, we have to fight for room for individuals to develop in freedom, but with responsibility. We cannot allow government to take power away from people without giving them adequate controls in return. The checks on power should have a secure institutional basis, but require the provision of a solid education, independent media and full access to information to function. These are the prerequisites of a strong democracy, where individuals retain power over their own lives. It is this vision that Social Liberals bring to our globalised future.

Liberalism and Globalisation

Graham Watson

To all previous generations, the major political challenges have been local, national, or involving part, but not all, of our world. Even the so-called 'world wars' of the twentieth century left many countries untouched. Our generation no longer enjoys such a limited constituency. While it remains true, as Tip O'Neill[19] said, that 'all politics is local', local now sometimes means local to our global village.

The expression 'global village' was coined to demonstrate the phenomenon of globalisation. Globalisation is about a world of inter-connected communities. Technology and the spread of language learning have transformed our ability to communicate. Exploration and the trade and investment which have followed have changed our economic perspectives and practices and have vastly increased wealth. Travel has opened new horizons and opportunities for human contact undreamt of by our forebears. Yet globalisation has not come without a cost. Criminals have organised global networks to a point where internationally organised crime has grown to pose a gargantuan threat. Human-driven damage to our natural environment threatens the future viability of human life on our planet. Powerlessness and alienation from government have restricted the opportunities for many individuals to employ that basic human instinct which is to develop their own abilities to improve their lot and that of their families and neighbours.

This essay looks at globalisation through the prism of liberal ideas. It does so against the background of the triumph in our generation of one world view over another, i.e. of the free or social market economy

---

[19] Congressman Tip O'Neill was Democrat Party leader and Speaker of the US House of Representatives from 1977-87.

over state socialism, which has done much to reduce armed conflict and to encourage the spread of democracy and the rule of law, the fundamentals of liberalism. It is inspired by the belief that human values are essentially the same in every community, that basic human needs and responses transcend race, religion or language-based culture. It concludes that the challenges to humankind require a new emphasis on and new approaches to global governance and that the management structures of our world must evolve to take account of this. Why? Because the communities of our world are not just inter-connected: we are interdependent. Herein lies our greatest challenge.

Let's Talk...

Most facets of humankind's inheritance from nature appear designed to assist the survival of the species. The striking exception to this, as George Steiner[20] has shown, is language. Mutual incomprehension has been used by the unscrupulous throughout the ages as an incitement to hatred and conflict. Physical barriers to communication, too, have limited the exchange of ideas. Yet the spread of English and Mandarin Chinese and, to a lesser, but nonetheless important extent, of Spanish - accompanied by the advent of the telephone, the recent discoveries of voice and image broadcasting and the remarkable development of the internet - have transformed humankind's ability to communicate.

A person on one side of the world can now see and talk to their counterpart on the other without setting foot outside their front door. A document can be sent from Berlin to Beijing in a nano-second. Disney and Pokemon characters appeal to children in east and west alike just as the pressures of parenthood unite their elders. Communication is now limited more by investment in networks, hardware and language teaching than by means of personal transport. Such investment must be a priority for liberals.

---

[20] George Steiner is an intellectual, linguist and author, notably of *The Tower of Babel.*

Triumphalism, however, must be avoided. Though few now believe that the courageous development of Esperanto could ever meet the expectations of its founders, however far-sighted in their day and age, the absence of a lingua franca remains a barrier to harmonious human relations. The demands of global governance will require vastly improved global communication, just as protection of our cultural inheritance requires us to combat the alarming decline of linguistic diversity. Much investment will be needed too in inter-cultural sensitivity. The shocking extent of racial hatred in most countries is a major barrier to peaceful communication and world development.

... and Work Together

The experience of liberalism in Europe in the eighteenth, nineteenth and twentieth centuries suggests that if our world were truly a village, rather more of its wealthier members would be shocked by the misery of the poor and motivated to self-sacrifice to provide for all what Ralf Dahrendorf[21] has called greater 'life chances'. Of the six billion human beings on our planet, half of them live on less than two euros a day and 800 million go to sleep hungry every night. Figures provided by the World Bank show that 80% of the world's population has only 20% of global GDP. Moreover, by the year 2025, the population will increase by one third, with most of the two billion new citizens living in the developing world. Such conditions create instability. Even those motivated essentially by self-interest can hardly ignore James Wolfensohn's[22] edict that development assistance is not charity, but a vital investment in global peace and security.

The market economy, intelligently regulated, is the most powerful instrument known to us to promote human development. That we have not yet learned to use it properly is clear from periodic international financial crises, local environmental devastation, the unchecked

---

[21] Ralf Dahrendorf is a Liberal philosopher, former German government minister, European Commissioner and now a Member of the House of Lords.
[22] James Wolfensohn is the President of the World Bank.

spread of preventable disease and the fear, insecurity and voicelessness of millions of people. The imperative for our generation must be to regard the phenomenon of globalisation as an opportunity and to use the market economy as a tool for social inclusion.

I am not suggesting, as some on the new left appear to, that there is no longer a role for government. The failure of the developed countries to meet the United Nations' target of spending 0.7% of GDP on development aid is currently depriving the poor of 100 billion euros per annum. It is almost certainly depriving them of far more in terms of the technical assistance and capacity building which would come with the private investment stimulated by such public aid. Development assistance is not a substitute for private investment, but a catalyst. Failure to provide it suggests, as Victor Gollancz[23] put it so starkly, that the inhabitants of wealthy countries prefer the death of those in the developing world to their own inconvenience. As J.K. Galbraith[24] has observed, aid will be most effective if it is targeted first and foremost on education and particularly the education of women.

Perhaps the greatest challenge for liberals, however, is reform of trade policy. Aid and debt relief without access to first world markets can be nothing more than a palliative. Tariff barriers to primary exports from developing countries are sometimes as high as 100%, while annual agricultural subsidies in industrialised countries exceed 300 billion euros. Even with a level playing field, developing countries will find it hard to compete. Currently they find it almost impossible.

If the grounds on which liberals must fight the right wing are those of greed and narrow self-interest, the so-called green movement must also be actively opposed by liberals for its resistance to scientific and technological progress. As the UN human development reports and similar studies consistently show, scientific advances have been the

---

[23] Victor Gollancz was the founder of the charity War on Want.
[24] John Kenneth Galbraith is a Liberal philosopher, university professor and author of many works. The one referred to here is *The Good Society*.

key to better nutrition, improved health and life expectancy and rising living standards in much of the developing world. Science and technology are vital tools for development, though lack of proper regulation, know-how and investment still dog attempts to employ them to best effect. While intermediate technology will remain the best route for some developing communities, others must not be starved of the full fruits of human inventiveness nor treated as a lucrative market for outdated western technology.

Human interchange

A modern day Marco Polo, travelling the silk road to China, would find his route barred regularly by armed men. Piri Reis and his crew would be turned away from western European ports[25]. The nineteenth and twentieth century concept of the nation state tends to impede the human interchange which has so enriched our society through the ages. Fear of invasion by foreign hordes is so frequently and effectively stoked up by nationalists that permission to enter a country seems dictated as often by irrational fear as by good sense.

Yet the number of human beings seeking to move from one country to another has hardly changed. The readiness of a small proportion of people in every society to up sticks, for reasons of political asylum, individual betterment or simply extended tourism, remains constant. Where immigration is not legally permitted it is nonetheless often attempted, frequently successfully and normally tolerated by the host country for reasons of the obvious economic benefits it brings.

The current western debate about immigration and asylum provides a key test for liberals in combating prejudice with prudence. The best example of policy response can be seen in Canada, where liberals' electoral success has been notable. Recognising that zero immigration is not a realistic policy option and that immigrants contribute hugely

---

[25] Marco Polo was an Italian overland adventurer, Piri Reis a Turkish sea captain and cartographer.

not only to their host communities but also (through remittance of money) to their countries of origin, the Canadian government has opened the 'front door' to legal immigration in order more effectively to combat the shocking new 'back door' slave trade of the illegal movement of people.

In stark contrast, Europe, Japan and the USA are still fumbling around for an effective policy response, while other, less wealthy, countries are left to bear the brunt of western indecision and sometimes to shoulder the burden of mass influx of people escaping famine, hunger or conflict. Yet developed countries need immigration to counter population decline. If charity and hospitality fail to dictate a more generous response from these countries, self-interest should. A significant beneficial side effect might be more effective moves to tackle racial prejudice and social disadvantage of ethnic minority communities, without which citizens of wealthy countries are likely to encounter growing difficulties in a world in which Caucasians are a minority.

International organised crime

The failure of international cooperation is perhaps nowhere more apparent than in the phenomenon of internationally organised crime. To paraphrase Mark Twain[26], the robbers are halfway round the world before the cops have got their boots on. International criminal gangs run a trade in customs fraud and in the smuggling of drugs, small arms and even weapons-grade plutonium which is highly lucrative. Sometimes they are more powerful, in their ability to control matters, than the national governments whose officials are too often bribed or terrorised into assisting them. The smuggling of people - usually, in the case of women and children, for the purposes of sexual slavery and paedophilia - is a recently discovered and particularly despicable aspect of their actions.

---

[26] Mark Twain, American author, wrote 'A lie is half way around the world before truth has got his boots on'.

The United Nations Organisation and other coordinating bodies have sought to persuade governments to coordinate their responses by improving cooperation between police forces and national judiciaries. Agreements struck, however, involve too little action, too late. Lack of political will and arguments about national sovereignty hamper cooperation between crime fighters just as the absence of internationally recognised warrants for arrest, the calling of witnesses or production of evidence hamper the prosecuting authorities.

The international drug trade is believed to be worth 8% of global GDP, the international trafficking of humans somewhere between 12 and 20 billion euros. Failure to agree effective global action against laundering of the profits and the finances of these trades through the world's financial and legal apparatus (which is perhaps the easiest way to combat such crime) is a striking indication of the impotence of the forces of law and order. Hence, the claim by national politicians facing election, that they can and will tackle crime effectively, is a lie and a sham by persons unprepared to engage in the pooling of national sovereignty necessary to protect their citizens from crime.

Environment

The need for global governance is perhaps nowhere clearer, at least to western European observers, than in the protection of our natural environment. Growing evidence collected by the International Panel on climate change, based on shrinking ice sheets, rising sea levels, changing weather patterns, migration of plants and animals and the increasing carbon content of air tells us that climate change is making our planet warmer than at any time in the past 10,000 years. This threatens our ability to provide food, water and shelter and threatens to bring suffering disproportionately to those who make their living from the land and the seas in the tropical and sub tropical parts of Asia, Africa and Latin America. Ironically, these people are those least responsible for human induced climate change.

The challenge is mammoth and there is no time to lose. Limiting and reducing the growing volume of gases (carbon dioxide, methane, nitrous oxide and others) which human beings and nature emit into the atmosphere will require a huge and concerted effort by government at all levels in all countries. The UN Convention on climate change, through its agreements in Rio de Janeiro, Kyoto and Bonn, has made a good start. But with the world's major polluter, the USA (four percent of the world's population, 25% of global emissions), in denial and others lukewarm, perhaps only an initiative such as the global Climate Community proposed by Christopher Layton[27] can carry momentum forward until political opinion everywhere has recognised the imperatives of survival beyond perceived challenges in the military sphere. In return for their farsightedness, members of this climate community would gain major competitive advantages through the energy efficiencies and sustainable technologies their industries would develop.

Global governance

From the Convention on International Trade in Endangered Species to the Permanent International Criminal Court for those guilty of crimes against humanity, the world community is reaching out for instruments to tackle the problems of our age. Yet it is in the failure of nation states to establish effective instruments of international government that the challenge to humankind resides. Where these have been established, nation state governments often appear unwilling to admit to their citizens that power can no longer effectively be exercised in national capitals and to explain fully and canvass support for the new arrangements which are made.

Most attempts at global governance have achieved only limited consensus, have been of Heath Robinson[28] design and have proven inadequate to the task. Only under current Secretary General Kofi

---

[27] Christopher Layton is a world federalist and author of, among many works, a recent pamphlet entitled *A Global Climate Community*.
[28] W. Heath Robinson, UK cartoonist, is famous for drawings depicting complicated mechanical devices for the performance of very simple tasks.

Annan has the United Nations, now some fifty years old, begun to be effective. The international financial institutions, with their poverty reduction strategies, could make a real difference if their wealthier members placed more emphasis on client involvement in action to solve problems and less on the 'Washington consensus' whereby they seek to dictate economic policies to the governments of developing countries. Military alliances, such as NATO, have often been effective in delivering policies agreed by their members but, by the limited nature of their membership, have been divisive and have more frequently contributed to global discord than brought harmony.

The North American Free Trade Agreement, the Organisation of American States, the Organisation of African Unity and attempts at economic cooperation in Asia have been useful vehicles to promote regional co-operation, just as some UN specialised agencies and conventions have advanced global dialogue. But progress has been slow and piecemeal and lacks any clear global framework or effective forum for public assent.

Indisputably, the best example of international governance, though hardly a shining one, is the European Union, where member states have voluntarily pooled sovereignty in a number of policy areas. Decision-making by Directive or Framework Regulation has allowed governments to respond faster to change than the laborious workings of international conventions. Scrutiny of legislation and administrative practice by the European Parliament has provided a degree of democratic legitimacy which should be the envy of many. It may be that western Europe has developed, unwittingly, a model for government on a wider scale.

The case against supranational democracy is that there does not yet exist a supranational polity, i.e. that citizens do not yet think of themselves essentially as global citizens and that, if they do, there is no consensus on any one model of government, let alone parliamentary democracy. If this is true, it is true to a far lesser degree than a generation ago. Few now believe it is possible to pull the blankets over their heads and wish that the world would go away. The onus of proof today rests on those who resist change rather than on its advocates.

Liberals point to the spread of democracy in the post-Cold War world and to growing pressure from citizens in undemocratic states for democratic government and the rule of law which extend beyond regular elections and carefully crafted legal texts. Totalitarian governments, now few in number, are increasingly the focus of organised dissent from their unenfranchised citizens and the campaign for universal judicial norms and standards spreads apace.

Yet we cannot claim a triumph for democracy in its current form. Even where national leaders have remained subject to effective democratic oversight and control by their national parliaments in matters of domestic policy, they generally evade such control over their common actions in bodies such as the G8 and the WTO. From Seattle to Prague, from Stockholm to Genoa, their actions are increasingly contested.

While violent protest remains limited to a small group of well trained, well organised and well financed anarchists, supported perhaps by those who profit from ineffective global governance, it draws support from a coalition of interests - from political opponents of capitalism to vested interests in labour unions - which oppose the leaders' common actions. Protest is joined by many who feel a growing sense of alienation from politics. Questioning the legitimacy of such summits, the protesters contend that democratic governments are no longer relevant, that their power has been usurped or their acquiescence purchased by multi-national businesses who increasingly rule the world. Official reaction to these protests, rather than attempting to understand and counter criticism, too often appears to start from the basis that the civil liberties the protesters enjoy inspire criminality.

Failure of political leaders to connect with popular sentiment will serve only to feed it. Until, as a spokesman for Belgium's Liberal led government pointed out, we have 'less technics, more politics' - in other words, until politicians regain and communicate a long term vision which transcends short term fixes - the violent protests look likely to continue. Not only must national leaders be prepared to conduct an open dialogue with the 'social fora', however, they may also need to be willing to adapt decision-making to the demands of the twenty-first century citizen who thinks both nationally and globally.

The more far-sighted representatives of what is known as 'international civil society' recognise the problems faced by national government in facing up to supranational challenges. They admit too, however, the lack of democratic legitimacy of single issue protest groups and they condemn violent protest. Slowly but surely, through a dialogue they have started with elected politicians, ideas for new forms of governance are beginning to emerge.

The dialogue ranges from the meetings of civil society which precede inter-governmental conferences to the recently established People's Assembly of the United Nations. In some policy areas it is already established - organisations such as GLOBE (Global Legislators for a Balanced Environment) have brought together lawmakers in environmental policy for nearly a decade. What is missing is an all-purpose international forum with democratic legitimacy.

Drawing on the experience of the EU in which decision making is shared between the heads of national governments (the Council) and directly elected representatives of the people, a proposal for an e-parliament, currently under discussion between politicians and pressure group representatives, seeks to link, electronically and otherwise, elected representatives from every country in a new 'earth parliament'. Though still in the gestation phase, such an assertion of universal democratic values may, in the words of American poet Ralph Waldo Emerson, 'fire a shot which will ring around the world'.

Attempts at organising a supranational democratic forum may be pie-in-the-sky politics, or they may be straws in the wind. Increasingly, however, citizens are mobilising to take control of their shared global destiny. Unless the heads of state and government of our world have the vision and the commitment to democratic forms of global governance such as that shown by the founders of the EU, and the courage and skill to convince their electorates of the need for it, it will grow organically beyond their control. Such is the power of the human spirit.

Managing Globalisation:
Concepts and Criteria for Liberal Governance

Jan-Kees Wiebenga

At the dawn of the 21st Century, Liberalism is on the rise. With the defeat of fascism in Europe and the collapse of communism, it seems obvious that Liberalism has become the dominant political ideology. This fact is well illustrated by the political slide in European left wing circles, with parties now split between those who wish to return to socialist ideals and those moving to the centre and to the right. Recently, a more liberal approach has been adopted by the various European socialist parties in power. Whether disguised under specious names such as 'the Third Way' or 'die Neue Mitte', essential liberal elements are easily recognisable in many instances.

Yet it is another related development which is the subject of this essay, in some aspects reflecting this Liberal 'victory': the ongoing process of globalisation. A broad term indeed: what is globalisation? More often than not, globalisation is characterised as bringing about new and revolutionary changes in international society and economy. Mankind is perceived to be on the verge of entering a 'connected world', an information-driven society. In that 'Tomorrow-land' some suggest that familiar social and political concepts will become irrelevant. There is, as one commentator noted, no longer a place for the 'reflexive twinges of national sovereignty'. The territorial state and its democratic system are to be things of the past.

However, this 'strong' definition of globalisation is not one I share. In my view, globalisation can be viewed as a positive development. Why? In its essence, it is liberal and it shows that liberal philosophy can work in a positive manner. Globalisation has two parameters: material policy and immaterial policy. The first is the economic aspect of the globalisation process, especially the ever expanding relationships of free trade between nation states; the rise of an international market in some aspects independent of the constraints of nation states or international organisations. Immaterial policy can be defined as that part of the globalisation process which is concerned with the organisation of socio-political structures. This relates to concepts such as human rights, multi-party democracy and the constitutional state. In these areas, the consequences of globalisation are even greater than in the purely economic sphere. All the more reason to study these concepts from a Liberal standpoint and its relationship to globalisation.

First and foremost, it must be clear that these concepts are an essential, indispensable part of Liberalism. In this respect, I would like to refer to Liberal values and the notion of cultural relativism. Are our Liberal values to be understood as absolute values? And universal? Philosophers and cultural relativists may quibble over such questions but the concept of human rights, multi-party democracy and rule of law as such cannot be negotiated. These are conditions for the humane development of man, of the individual. This also goes for the basic system underlying the material aspect, namely a market economy. Moreover, the connection between the economic aspect of globalisation and Liberal values is clear. The market economy provides a basis, a vital underpinning for democracy and human rights, providing citizens with the means and the opportunities to take part in the democratic process. In short, both aspects of globalisation are intertwined, and cannot be seen as separate.

The Liberal challenge is to assure that globalisation remains orientated in a positive direction and that the essential underpinning Liberal values are not undermined in the process. Those who support the thesis of 'strong' globalisation feel that it is precisely this process which is undermining longstanding socio-political concepts, including our Liberal values. Thus the crucial questions are of how to advance these Liberal concepts in a globalising world and how to ensure a positive development within the globalisation paradigm. In attempting to answer these questions, one immediately stumbles upon two fundamental problems. The first is that our liberal ideals are specifically Western concepts and the second that there exist states and societies which do not accept these concepts.

Democracy, human rights and the modern state have their origins in a certain historic period and place, arguably the European Enlightenment and the French Revolution. The first saw the birth of individualism and with the advent of the second the fundaments for democracy and the constitutional state were laid. As noted, there are countries that do not accept such philosophical concepts and their political implications. Yet, it is precisely globalisation which forces the confrontation with concepts such as democracy, human rights and the rule of law in countries which do not currently accept the practise of these liberal concepts.

The reaction of these states reflects the curious all-encompassing reach of the various globalisation processes. In some cases, there has been an awkward combination of adaptation to the new economic and political circumstances, incremental change and opening-up, and dismissive self-isolation. A stance which is remarkably parallel to the way the relationships of free trade are handled by all nations within the World Trade Organisation. Even those most ardent advocates of trade liberalisation are held back in various sectors by national protectionist interests. Yet those countries which are ideologically furthest from the globalisation agenda are forced into making choices they may not want to make. One example is China. It is impossible to escape the influence of global television and the internet, so external pressure on China concerning human rights issues is continual. The participation of China's economy in the contemporary international economic system and its accession to the WTO, further accentuates this process.

Cases such as China, of course, lead to difficulties concerning the advancement of our liberal and democratic ideals. One way to resolve these difficulties is to push through the promotion of Western concepts as a stipulation prior to economic engagement in fora such as the WTO. For a truly effective promotion of democracy, human rights and the constitutional state, a different approach is needed: the approach of committed dialogue. This is a fruitful path to take because one of the most important aspects of globalisation is the necessity of co-operation between different groups. A truly modern approach is required, that of dialogue between citizens, be it in intensive communication through electronic means, through international civil society groups or through something as simple as tourism. Liberals can contribute to such a dialogue by stressing the worth of the above-named concepts and by listening to the arguments of the other parties involved. This is the best way to ensure the development of democracy, human rights and the constitutional state in the globalising world. Such co-operation and dialogue are, and will remain, highly preferable to mechanisms such as boycotts, isolation and the use of force. In the long run, the hope must be that these concepts can be introduced and discussed, and that slowly but surely they will be adopted.

Naturally, in meeting the challenge of globalisation, more is needed than the affirmation and spreading of the concepts outlined above. Here Europe provides us with a fine model for a modern Liberal project - free movement of persons, capital, goods and services are key objectives for the European Union, though much remains to be done. Foremost, the practical implementation of Liberal concepts must be stepped up so as to ensure a positive development of globalisation. Criteria for a European Liberal program can be formulated into criteria for Liberal 'governance'. I would like to mention three points.

First is the need for political reform. The fall of the Santer Commission in March 1999 provides a spectacular example in terms of the constitutional development of the EU, for which the ELDR group can proudly claim the major responsibility. The ELDR group introduced the concept of individual censure of a Commissioner in a draft resolution (the Commissioner mentioned being Edith Cresson, former Prime Minister of France). Due to the controversy of Commissioner Cresson refusing to resign individually, amongst other complications, the whole Commission finally stepped down collectively. Since this scandal and the reformist efforts of the European Liberals, the idea of the political accountability of all Commissioners to the European Parliament has been widely accepted. Under this subheading of political reform, it can also be pointed out that the Liberals are at the forefront of the wider European bureaucracy reform process by pressing for greater transparency. Arguably, the EU does not fulfil its own membership criteria applied to the candidate countries in Central and Eastern Europe with regards to its own democratic legitimacy, particularly in terms of the implementation of concepts such as public participation. Political accountability, transparency in governance and democratic control are absolute necessities. They are also core Liberal values.

A radical decentralisation of the European Union could be a second element to this program, given that a debate on the EU's core tasks is gathering momentum. More so than the other political groups, the Liberals have always supported the concept of a small but well-organised executive power. This means that we should stop talking about attribution of new tasks to the EU's institutions. Rather, we should rather try to promote the principle of subsidiarity. The EU's agricultural policy and the different European structural funds are centrally controlled at present. Both would benefit from decentralisation, even more so in view of the coming enlargement process. The EU should deal with the fight against the trafficking of drugs, but not with the fight against local crime. It should deal with the international exchange of students and academics, but not with primary education and so on. The key point here is that a continual dialogue on the manner in which Government is run, the responsibilities and competencies of governance at European level, is needed to ensure the legitimacy of democracy and the state.

The fight against corruption should be placed high on the Liberal agenda. It is heart-breaking to see how authoritarianism still rules in parts of the Third World and in parts of Eastern Europe, but it is also true that democracies, including European Union member states, are unfortunately not entirely free from corruption either. Authoritarian regimes and corruption are closely related and so here we may reflect upon a core Liberal belief: open societies with a maximum participation of all stakeholders ensure a transparency that does not allow any room for corruption. It is the rule of law which both ensures the freedom of actors and constitutes the enabling framework. Here too one sees the connection with the demands of globalisation. A stable balance between material and immaterial globalisation is required. Corruption gnaws at the foundations of both.

These items are classic Liberal priorities indeed. But they have not lost their urgency, either in Europe or on a global scale. For liberals, the promotion of these criteria and the underlying concepts are the most important tasks at hand.

It is clear that Liberalism is the future. The current trend of globalisation shows us this much. The EU is a Liberal project embodying a combination of democracy, human rights and the market economy. All in all, the EU is seen by many outsiders as a bright star in a rather dark world, combining concepts and criteria which no country meeting the challenge of globalisation can do without.

So Liberals have to promote the export of this model of peaceful economic and political co-operation, based on central Liberal concepts, to the various regions of the world. Much of Asia, for instance, works on the concept of a market economy and, whilst the concept of democracy is underdeveloped, plurilateral efforts with respect to regional trading blocs and the muted initiative to form an Asian Development Fund indicate that opening up is the trend. Africa is still far away from Liberalism and so very much has to be done in this respect. Yet it is precisely through engagement on Liberal principles of trade and development assistance that changes will be brought about. In his Inaugural Address (January 1961) John F. Kennedy said, "In the long history of this world, only a few generations have been granted the role of defending freedom in its hour of maximum danger. I do not shrink from this responsibility. I welcome it". He said this in the midst of the Cold War. The Cold War is over. But promoting Liberalism in our times remains a great challenge and a necessity.

Further Reading and Web Resources

<u>Resources on Liberalism</u>

The European Liberal Democrats
http://eld.europarl.eu.int/

The European Parliament
http://www.europarl.eu.int/

World Liberalism
http://www.worldlib.org

<u>Further Reading on Globalisation</u>

Globalisation - General

Barnet, R and Cavanagh, J. (1996) 'The Homogenisation of Global Culture' in Mander, J and Goldsmith, E. (eds) (1996) *The Case Against the Global Economy and For a Turn Toward the Local*, San Francisco, Sierra Club Books.

Henderson, H. (1996) *Building a Win-Win World: Life Beyond Global Economic Warfare,* San Francisco, Berrett-Koehler Publishers.

Mander, J and Goldsmith, E. (eds) (1996) *The Case Against the Global Economy and For a Turn Toward the Local*, San Francisco, Sierra Club Books.

Martin, H.P & Schuman, H. (1996) *The Global Trap: Globalisation and the Assault on Democracy and Prosperity*, London, Zed Books.

Rodrick, D. (1997) *Has Globalisation Gone Too Far?* Washington, Institute for International Economics.

Free trade ideology, development and environment

Beder, S. (1997) *Global Spin: The Corporate Assault on the Environment,* Dartington, Green Books.

Bhagwati, J. (1988) *Protectionism*, Cambridge, Massachusetts, The MIT Press.

Bhaskar,V & Glyn, A. (1995) *The North, The South and the Environment: Ecological Constraints and the Global Economy*, London, Earthscan.

Carley, M & Spapens, P. (1998) *Sharing the World: Sustainable Living and Global Equity in the 21st Century,* London, Earthscan.

Caufield, C. (1996) *Masters of Illusion: The World Bank and the Poverty of Nations,* London, Macmillan.

Chossudovsky, M. (1997) *The Globalisation of Poverty: Impacts of IMF and World Bank Reforms,* Penang, Malaysia, Third World Network.

Collins, J and Lear, J. (1996) *Free Market Miracle or Myth? Chile's Neo-Liberal Experiment,* The Ecologist, 26 (4): 156-166.

Douthwaite, R. (1992) *The Growth Illusion: How Economic Growth Has Enriched the Few, Impoverished the Many, and Endangered the Planet,* Bideford, Devon, Green Books.

Gray, H.P. (1985) *Free Trade or Protection? A Pragmatic Analysis,* London, Macmillan.

Greider, W. (1997) *One World Ready or Not: The Manic Logic of Global Capitalism,* London. Penguin Books Ltd.

French, H.F. (1998) 'Assessing Private Capital Flows to Developing Countries' in Brown, L.R. (ed) (1998) *State of the World 1998: A*

Worldwatch Institute Report on Progress Towards a Sustainable Society, London, Earthscan.

Jackson, J.H. (1998) *The World Trade Organisation: Constitution and Jurisprudence,* London, Royal Institute of International Affairs.

Jacobs, M. (ed). (1996) *The Politics of the Real World,* London, Earthscan.

Jepma, C.J, Jager, H. and Kamphuis, E. (1996) *Introduction to International Economics,* London, Longman.

Korten, D. (1995) *When Corporations Rule the World,* London, Earthscan.

Krugman, P. (1996) *Pop Internationalism,* Cambridge, Massachusetts, The MIT Press.

Lang, T and Hines, C. (1993) *The New Protectionism: Protecting the Future Against Free Trade,* London, Earthscan.

Lanjouw, G.J. (1995) *International Trade Institutions,* London, Longman.

McCord, N. (1970) *Free Trade: Theory and Practice from Adam Smith to Keynes,* Newton Abbott, Devon, David and Charles Ltd.

Mishan, E.J. (1993) *The Costs of Economic Growth,* London, Weidenfeld and Nicholson.

Repetto, R. (1994) *Trade and Sustainable Development: A Report for UNEP by Robert Repetto of WRI,* New York, United Nations Environment Programme (UNEP).

TWN. (1994) *The World Trade Organisation: Trade and Environment Position Paper of the Third World Network,* Penang, Malaysia, Third World Network.

Web Resources on Globalisation

Civil Society Groups / Non Governmental Organisations (NGOs)

Corporate Europe Observatory
http://www.xs4all.nl/~ceo/

Fairtrade Foundation
http://www.fairtrade.org.uk/

Friends of the Earth The Citizens' Guide to Trade, Environment and Sustainability
http://www.foei.org/activist_guide/tradeweb/index.htm

Third World Network
http://www.twnside.org.sg/

World Development Movement
http://www.wdm.org.uk/

Free Trade Think Tanks

The Adam Smith Institute
http://www.adamsmith.org.uk/

Cato Centre for Trade Policy Studies
http://www.freetrade.org/

General Information

Center for International Development at Harvard University - provides information and research papers on international trade policy: http://www.cid.harvard.edu/cidtrade/

International trade law links
http://www.stcl.edu/currents/tradelawlinks.html

International Institutions

United Nations Commission on Sustainable Development (UNCSD)
http://www.un.org/esa/sustdev/csd.htm

United Nations Conference on Trade and Development (UNCTAD)
http://www.unctad.org/

United Nations Development Programme (UNDP)
http://www.undp.org/

World Business Council for Sustainable Development
http://www.wbcsd.ch/

The World Trade Organisation
http://www.wto.org/

New Ideas for a New Century

"The Centre is a public policy think tank, pursuing the values of the Liberal Democrats, but open to all those who wish to debate social, economic and political reform."

The Aims of the Centre for Reform

The views expressed in this pamphlet are the views of the authors. They are not necessarily shared by individual Trustees, members of the Advisory Board, members of the Management Committee, or the Director. Authors are not necessarily members of the Liberal Democrats, and Centre for Reform pamphlets do not constitute Liberal Democrat policy.